# Navajo
# Kinship and
# Marriage

# NAVAJO

**Gary Witherspoon**

# KINSHIP AND MARRIAGE

The University of Chicago Press

*Chicago and London*

The University of Chicago Press, Chicago 60637
The University of Chicago Press, Ltd., London

**Library of Congress Cataloging in Publication Data**

Witherspoon, Gary.
  Navajo kinship and marriage.

  Bibliography: p.
  Includes index.
  1. Navaho Indians—Social life and customs.
2. Kinship—Southwest, New.   I. Title.
E99.N3W68   301.42'1'0979   74-21340
ISBN 0-226-90417-2

# Contents

# Foreword

The Navajo are one of the most studied people in the world; yet their social organization is one of the least well understood. A little-studied people may seem to be well understood. But a much-studied people like the Navajo provide a wealth of material from a variety of different observers over a long period of time, and so gaps, discrepancies, and contradictions between reports and reporters become evident.

These gaps, discrepancies, and contradictions derive in part from the different aims and methods of the different reporters. For different reporters use different theoretical schemes in terms of which to make and to report their observations, and different theories require different kinds of data.

Today's facts are not simply a new set of "facts," hitherto "undiscovered," but are instead—as are all facts—statements made within the framework of a conceptual scheme and are only meaningful as such.

How good our understanding of Navajo social organization is, then, depends on the theoretical tools in terms of which the observations are made, analyzed, and presented. And it is on both these scores that I think Dr. Witherspoon's book will stand for a long time as the definitive statement of Navajo kinship and marriage. For he has wedded a new, carefully developed, precisely defined theoretical framework to an extraordinarily high quality of observational material.

Dr. Witherspoon's theoretical scheme uses a sharp, well-defined conception of "culture," one which is narrower but far more precise and powerful than that usually used. He distinguishes "culture," patterns *for* behavior treated as a system of symbols and meanings, from patterns *of* behavior, the system of social relations as it can actually be observed. It is in terms of the former that the latter can be understood by those who act as well as by the observer of the actions. Social action is thus a meaningful system and a system which depends on meaning, and the observer's task is not simply to report on what the Navajo do, but also on what it means to the Navajo when they do what they do.

However powerful such a theoretical scheme may be, it is nothing if it is not based on perceptive, accurate, understood observations, which depend on establishing what the Navajo mean when they act.

It is on this ground too, that Dr. Witherspoon's book will be considered the definitive work on Navajo kinship and marriage. For Dr. Witherspoon brings a long, close association with the Navajo to bear on providing the observational base for this book. He has lived for a long time with the Navajo, speaks the language fluently, and has a wide network of kinsmen among the Navajo through his wife and children, in addition to his training as an anthropologist.

These unusual qualifications, which most observers of the Navajo have lacked, assure the reader of the likelihood of one more very important quality in this book. He provides the reader with an account of the Navajo's own conceptions of their cultural units and their interrelations. The reader does not get the Navajo forced into those procrustean beds suitable for comparative sociological analysis but totally unsuited to any understanding of Navajo culture as the Navajo themselves conceive of it.

The comparative frame does not necessarily lead to the erection of totally unsuitable comparative categories, but it is certainly prone to that disability, for it has developed a long, tedious string of such categories which are not often checked against the natives' own cultural categories.

If we are assured of anything, then, it is that this book is more likely to represent the Navajo description of their cultural universe as the Navajo conceive of it than most of the work we have had heretofore. Not only because of the fact that Dr. Witherspoon is so closely involved and related to them, but also because one of the cornerstones of his theoretical orientation is precisely to provide just that.

It is nice, for a change, to have a book about Navajo culture that is about Navajo culture—not the culture of the anthropologist—by someone who understands it.

David M. Schneider

# Preface

Major studies of Navajo social life began with the work of Gladys Reichard. Her first major study, *Social Life of the Navajo Indians*, published in 1928, was a general ethnographic account covering kin terms, dyadic relationships, descent groups, marriage rules, and minor ceremonies. In 1939, Malcolm Carr Collier, Katherine Spencer, and Doraine Woolley reported on a study of Navajo clan and marriage practices at Pueblo Alto, New Mexico. At approximately the same time, Walter Dyk published a Navajo autobiography, *The Son of Old Man Hat* (1938), which contains some of the finest material available on Navajo social life.

In terms of anthropological interest in, and work with, the Navajo, the 1940s and 1950s might be characterized as the Kluckhohn era. The advent of Clyde Kluckhohn and his many colleagues and students flooded the Navajo reservation with fieldworkers and filled the files and shelves of the Peabody Museum with field notes and monographs on various aspects of Navajo culture. If Kluckhohn's life and work spearheaded interest in the Navajo, his untimely death in 1960 did not leave a vacuum. The Navajo field of investigation remains crowded when compared with that of other tribes and peoples. One of the standard jokes in anthropological circles is that the typical Navajo family contains a father, a mother, children, and an anthropologist.

Kluckhohn was relatively uninterested in kinship and social organization, and it seems that this lack of interest extended to many of his students and colleagues. More recently, however, greater attention has been given to Navajo kinship and social organization. David Aberle has taken the lead in this regard, followed by Mary Shepardson, Blodwen Hammond, Louise Lamphere, William Adams, James Downs, and Jerrold Levy. Although adding greatly to our understanding of Navajo social life, the increased attention and the additional data resulting from this attention have also produced a number of contradictions which have added to the confusion about Navajo kinship and social organization. David Aberle comments on this situation:

> Anthropologists who work among the Navajo sometimes comment on a certain "fuzzy" quality about their culture. And anthropologists who have not worked among the Navajo sometimes complain in exasperation about the "sloppy" field work which has thus far failed to define a large number of patterns with any clarity . . .
> This "fuzzy" quality seems to be largely manifested in social organization. . . . (1963: 1-2.)

I became intensely involved in Navajo social life six years before becoming a student of anthropology and before reading any written accounts of Navajo social life. Although this involvement in, and exposure to, Navajo social life was not experienced for the purpose of making analyses and descriptions of Navajo social life, much of the information contained in this book is based on those experiences and many others which have occurred since my initial exposure to anthropology in 1968.

Although it might properly be said that this book is based more on field experience than on fieldwork, I did make a rather thorough survey of social organization in the Rough Rock–Black Mountain area, and Part II of this book is based primarily on the results of that survey. The survey was initiated during my two years (1966-68) of work in community-school relations at the Rough Rock Demonstration School. The survey was later completed during my tenure as a graduate student in the department of anthropology at the University of Chicago.

A major aspect of my theoretical orientation to the subject matter of this book is to separate the actual patterns "of" behavior from the ideal patterns "for" behavior. Part I of this book discusses the conceptual framework and ideas which guide and order Navajo behavior but which are distinct from it. Part II deals with actual patterns of social organization and behavior, and illustrates how these behavioral and organizational patterns become more comprehensible and interpretable when the rules, ideas, and conceptual framework which underly them are understood. It would be difficult, if not impossible, for a foreign anthropologist unfamiliar with American football correctly to comprehend and describe the social behavior involved in playing a football game without consulting the rule book according to which the game is supposed to be played. Likewise, Navajo social life will remain an enigma if we do not consult the conceptual framework and rules on which it is based. Much of the confusion and contradiction found in descriptions of Navajo social life are due to a failure to distinguish the ideal from the actual, the rule from the exception, the social from the cultural.

Many anthropologists make studies of systems of kinship and marriage with too many questions answered before they get to the field. They already know that kinship is the apprehension or misapprehension of genealogical relationships, that kinsmen are not affines and that affines are not kinsmen, that matriliny is matriliny, that residence is either patrilocal, matrilocal, neolocal, or some variation of these, that father-child and mother-child are both relationships of the first order, and that egoism is the opposite of altruism. I try to avoid molding the Navajo system of kinship and marriage into the standard anthropological categories. Instead, I attempt to inspect and reveal the Navajo system according to its own features, exposing both its uniqueness and its regularity.

In expressing gratitude to those who assisted me with this book, first thanks must go to the many Navajo who have patiently and kindly taught me about their culture and social life. Those who assisted me most directly in putting together the cultural analysis of Navajo kinship were John Honie, John Caboni, Ray Winnie, Hasbah Yazzie, Rita Wheeler, Joe Begay, John Dick, and my wife and her family.

Nearly everyone within the fifty contiguous subsistence residential units which I studied helped provide the data for the social analysis. To all these wonderful people, I wish to extend my deepest affection and gratitude. The description of the social system at Rough Rock is not a study of human subjects; it is a respectful account of my friends. Wherever the mutual trust and respect of friendship conflicted with anthropological interests and goals, my friendship with the people took priority over anthropological concerns.

I wish also to express my appreciation to the entire community (students, faculty, and staff) of anthropologists at the University of Chicago. Discussions with Michael Moffatt, Raymond DeMallie, David Labby, and Ellen Becker were particularly helpful. Study with Fred Eggan, David Schneider, Victor Turner, Sol Tax, Ray

Fogelson, Paul Friedrich, and Clifford Geertz was highly stimulating. I wish to extend my thanks to all these members of the faculty.

In addition, I wish to express special thanks to Fred Eggan and David Schneider for their numerous helpful comments and criticisms on the first draft of this work. In addition, special thanks go to David Schneider for his assistance and encouragement while I was revising the original draft and preparing it for publication. I wish also to express my appreciation to Susan Sanford for doing the illustrations found in this book.

*Note on Spelling*

In accordance with the preferred usage of the Navajo Nation, the letter *j* has been used in the spelling of Navajo throughout this study, both in my own text and in quoted passages from other authors. Because of printing costs, the tonal marks over vowels in Navajo orthography have not been included. Otherwise, the recently standardized Navajo orthography has been followed in the spelling of Navajo words.

# 1 Navajo Kinship as a Cultural System

# 1     Kinship as a Cultural System

The title of this chapter is closely related to that of an article by Clifford Geertz, "Religion as a Cultural System." Geertz (1966: 3) states that his article refers to "the cultural dimension of religious analysis." The entire part I of this book is concerned with the cultural dimension of kinship analysis. Because the words "culture" and "kinship" have had many and varied uses and applications, a definition of these terms and their relationship to each other provide the content of chapter 1 and the necessary starting point of part I.

It is important to distinguish the cultural system from the social system. Until recently many anthropologists and sociologists have failed to make sharp distinctions between culture and society. Many times the concepts of social system or society and cultural system or culture were (and still are in some quarters) used almost interchangeably. This lack of distinction between the two led many social scientists to coin and employ the phrase "sociocultural" or "sociocultural complex." Because these terms have both folk and scientific meanings and are used by both lay and professional analysts, a discussion of their exact definitions might well begin with experiences and institutions common to the backgrounds of most readers of this work.

A well-known and broadly publicized activity in America is football. Football has both cultural and social dimensions, and provides a good example of each. For the purposes of this discussion, the cultural and social dimensions of the sport will be confined to the field where the games take place, even though there are of course interesting off-the-field aspects to teams and players.

The field is the universe or world within which action occurs. The actual playing of a football game within this field or universe is a social event, involving the interaction of at least twenty-two persons, who are divided into two groups. This social interaction constitutes the social dimension or social system of the game. The formations employed in the playing of the game might be used as examples of social structure. The way in which the activities of blocking, passing, running, kicking, and tackling are organized among the players is an example of social organization.

The various types of formations (social structures) employed and the organization of various duties assigned to players in these formations (social organization) might constitute a suitable area of inquiry by social scientists. Social scientists might discover that, under the conditions of fourth down and twenty yards to go on a team's own ten-yard line, the social structure often called "punt formation" makes the best adaptation to these environmental conditions. Ecological determinists might say that these environmental conditions cause the adoption of the punt-formation structural arrangement. Other social scientists might observe that, under the same conditions, with one additional variant—the team is behind by two touchdowns, and there are only two minutes left in the fourth quarter—the punt-formation social structure is not a good adaptation for social survival.

The discussion of the many factors and variants involved in the interaction of the social system of football could go on and on. In fact, the focus of the work of many social anthropologists and sociologists is concerned mainly with an analysis of social interaction such as that which occurs in football games. There is, however, one important element missing in this kind of focus and analysis. It is, as might have been anticipated, the cultural element or dimension.

There is a cultural dimension to football. Here social interaction takes place in an environment which is culturally defined and structured, and the interaction is ordered by a set of culturally derived rules. In fact, the rule book of football identifies and defines the elements of the game, explains the nature of the game, outlines the various elements and combinations possible in playing the game, and structures the relationship between the elements of the game.

This rule book (culture) defines the length and width of the field, the size and weight of the ball, the number of yards between stripes, the distance between the goals, and so on. It establishes the means a team may employ to reach its goals, the formations possible, the number of yards to be gained in order to get a first down, when and how the football can be kicked or passed, and so on. The rule book also defines the possible proper roles of various kinds of players, coaches, and officials. It contains sanctions to be inflicted upon those who violate the rules. In other words, the rule book (culture) creates the world or environment in which the game (social system) takes place. A cultural system is as necessary for the operation of a social system as the rule book is a necessary prerequisite for a football game.

The definition of culture as seen in football has its roots in some theories put forth by Emile Durkheim in the latter part of the nineteenth century. The rule book in football is somewhat analogous to what Durkheim called the collective conscience:

> The totality of beliefs and sentiments common to average citizens of the same society forms a determinate system which has its own life; one may call it the "collective" or "common conscience." No doubt, it has not a specific organ as a substratum; it is, by definition, diffuse in every reach of society. Nevertheless, it has specific characteristics which make it a distinct reality. It is, in effect, independent of the particular conditions in which individuals are placed; they pass on and it remains. . . . It is, thus, an entirely different thing from particular consciences, although it can be realized only through them. (1933: 70–80.)

At the beginning of his article "Religion as a Cultural System," Geertz provides an interesting quote from Santayana:

> Every living and healthy religion has a marked idiosyncrasy. Its power consists in its special and surprising message and in the bias which that revelation gives to life. The vistas it opens and the mysteries it propounds are another world to live in. . . . (1966: 1.)

The phrase "another world to live in" is significant because it indicates that religion, as a cultural system, creates the world for its adherents. Geertz explains that for anthropologists "the importance of religion lies in its capacity to serve . . . as a source of general, yet distinctive conceptions of the world, the self, and the relations between them . . ." (1966: 40.)

One common element in Durkheim's "collective conscience," Lévi-Strauss's "arbitrary system of representations" (1963: 49), Leach's "organizational ideas" (1961: 2), Schneider's "culture" (1968: 1–12), Santayana's "another world," Geertz's "distinctive conceptions of the world," Turner's "ideological systems controlling social relationships" (1966: 82), and my rule-book analogy is that they all exist on the conceptual level, not on the empirical level. They are not actual social relations. Regardless of what each of these writers thinks it consists of, and how it ought to be defined and described, there seems to be agreement on the point that there is a set of beliefs, concepts, ideas, views, and attitudes about the universe of action, being, and emotion which orders human behavior but is distinct from it. The term "culture" will be utilized in this volume, although it will be defined somewhat differently from the way any of those named above define it.

Having distinguished the cultural system from the social system, I shall now describe the constituent elements of the cultural system. Culture (1) identifies and defines the components of the universe of action, being, and emotion; (2) categorizes the components of the universe into domains, subdomains, divisions, subdivisions, and so on; (3) structures relationships between and among the components and component categories; (4) explains the nature and meaning of the components and component categories; and (5) relates the rules governing the moral order and organizational pattern of the universe. A discussion of each of these aspects of culture follows.

By identifying and defining the components of the universe, cultural systems, in one sense, create the universe. Cultural concepts do not just (or even necessarily) identify and define what really exists in the objective world, for reality itself is culturally defined. For example, ghosts may exist in one culturally defined world and not in another. Various gods exist in specific cultures but not in others. Harmful bacteria exist in one culturally defined world but not in another.

Each culture has an epistemological system by which various entities can be identified and defined. Proof of the existence of something is determined in different ways in various cultures. In one culture, the word of God or his prophets define what is real; in other cultures, diviners and mythological narratives determine the constitution of the world; and in still other cultures, objective methods based on materialistic assumptions define reality. To be sure, all cultural beliefs are validated in one degree or another by sensual experiences. But what is a valid sensual experience with real supernatural beings to one epistemological system is a figment of the imagination, an illusion of the mind, or a hallucination of the psyche to another. The nature and function of epistemological systems in cultural definitions of reality are infinitely more complex than these simple examples illustrate. Epistemology is mentioned here only to identify it with the cultural system and to suggest its importance.

Cultures categorize the components of the culturally defined universe in an infinite number of ways. Lévi-Strauss has written nearly an entire book, *The Savage Mind*, about various categorical schemes employed by peoples across the globe in classifying the components of their worlds. Lévi-Strauss even attempts a description of the logical structure by which conceptual categories of environmental phenomena are developed:

> A logical structure—initially a simple opposition—thus fans out in two directions: one abstract, in the form of a numerology, and the other concrete, first of elements and then of species. On each level semantic short-circuits permit direct connections with the level farthest away. The level of species, which is also the most particularized of those we have considered, does not, however, constitute a sort of limit or stopping point of the system: The latter does not fall into inertia but continues to progress through new detotalizations and retotalizations which can take place on several planes. (1966: 146-47.)

The numerous subcategories, categories, subclasses, classes, divisions, and domains of cultural categorization are extremely extensive and complex. An individual cultural anthropologist or linguist can study only a small and selected part of the total set of cultural categories which exist in a given culture.

Cultural systems also structure the relationships between and among the components and component categories of the culturally defined universe. These structural relationships may take numerous forms, such as one being the cause of another, or a part of another, or the source of another, or the opposite of another, and so on. Cultural entitites and categories may also be arranged either in hierarchical or equalitarian terms or in encompassing or complementary terms. Thus there are numerous kinds and types of structural arrangements possible between two components or categories. The greater structures which result from these primary connections have many more possible arrangements and dimensions, even though Lévi-Strauss has identified a basic structural pattern of cultural concepts:

> Starting from a binary opposition, which affords the simplest possible example of a system, this construction proceeds by the

aggregation, at each of the poles, of new terms, chosen because they stand in relations of opposition, correlation or analogy to it. (1966: 161.)

Culture also explains the nature and meaning of the components and component categories of the universe. Numerous and varied items, objects, concepts, acts, and beings are held to be sacred in various cultures. Still other kinds of things are defined as dangerous. Some objects and acts (rituals) are used to heal; others, for food, heat, clothing, and so on. Special value is placed on some things, while others are viewed as little more than worthless. There is an amazing lack of correlation with regard to the culturally defined natures of the same objects in the numerous cultures of the world. In one culture, a particular animal may be sacred and not eaten, while the same animal is eaten, or feared, or used as medicine in still other cultures. Any examination of the nature and uses of various items in the cultures of the world would clearly illustrate how the nature and meaning of a particular item are independently defined in each culture.

Cultures also relate the rules governing the moral order and organizational pattern of the universe. Both primitive and scientific thought and theory are founded on the need to create order out of chaos, links between the unlinked, relationships among the unrelated, structure in the unstructured, pattern for the unpatterned, attachments for the unattached, and places for the unplaced. Lévi-Strauss states that totemic beliefs which relate social groups to natural phenomena do not imply relationships of substance but "are allied to other beliefs and practices, directly or indirectly linked to classificatory schemes which allow the natural and social universe to be grasped as an organized whole." (1966: 135.)

The Navajo concept of "hozhǫ" refers to that state of affairs where everything is in its proper place and functioning in harmonious relationship to everything else. Such a condition specifies beauty as well. The Navajo often say "shił hozhǫ" which means "With me there is beauty, happiness, and harmony"—in other words, "Things in my world are in proper place and harmonious order." When this order is disrupted, sickness arises and must be treated by a restructuring of the harmonious order of the world. Navajo ceremonies re-create and restructure the universe for the patient, putting everything back in its proper place. Lévi-Strauss comments on this same matter:

A native thinker makes the penetrating comment that "All sacred things have their place" (Fletcher 2, p. 34). It could be said that being in their place is what makes them sacred for if they were taken out of their place, even in thought, the entire order of the universe would be destroyed. Sacred objects therefore contribute to the maintenance of order in the universe by occupying the places allocated to them. Examined superficially and from the outside, the refinements of ritual can appear pointless. They are explicable by a concern for what one might call "micro-adjustment"—the concern to assign every single creature, object or feature to a place within a class. (1966: 10.)

The culturally related moral order and organizational pattern of the universe form a coherent whole, based on the interrelatedness of all components and component categories of which the universe is constituted. This order and organization are described as moral because they portray the proper state of affairs—that is, the way things ought to be. As culture is a conceptual system, the moral order of the universe is a conceptual order, not an empirical fact. Men can tolerate and endure chaos in their social systems, but demand order in their cultural systems. The cultural conception of the universe is thus a unified, integrated, ordered, and coherent whole.

Cultural conceptions of, and attitudes toward, the world are embodied in symbols. The craving for symbols and the impulse to create and use them are integral to the life of man and his cultures. The mind seeks to express its concepts, ideas, and sentiments, and to see these embodied in objective symbols or symbolic acts. Man is a poet by birth:

> And, as imagination bodies forth
> The forms of things unknown, the poet's pen
> Turns them to shapes, and gives to airy nothing
> A local habitation and a name.
>
> (*A Midsummer Night's Dream*, Act V, Scene I.)

What the poet does in words and rhyme, groups of men do in symbolic acts and creations. Symbols capture and express, frame and focus, recall and retain, synthesize and condense cultural beliefs of enormous proportions into simple symbols which are polysemous and multivocal.

Symbols have two aspects or poles. On the one side, there is the substance of the objective symbol or the form of the symbolic act.

This aspect of symbols is related to the physical, the objective, the material, the organic, and the natural realms of experience and being. The other aspect of symbols can be found in the meanings they contain, the beliefs they express, the attitudes they focus, and the thoughts they capture. This second aspect or pole of symbols relates to the mental, the subjective, the immaterial, the super-organic, and the supernatural realms of experience and being. There are numerous other important aspects and qualities of symbols, but this brief description will suffice for the purposes of this chapter.

Kinship seems to be a universal cultural belief. Cultural concepts about kinship identify and define who is a kinsman. The criteria used in defining who is a kinsman vary widely in the cultures of the world. In American culture, kinsmen are those who are relatives by blood or by marriage (Schneider 1968: 21). In other cultures, those who would not be related according to the biogenetic categories of American kinship are indeed kinsmen. Some cultures restrict kinship to human beings, while others consider various animals, natural phenomena, and supernatural beings to be kinsmen. A kinsman is culturally defined and determined in each culture, even though some anthropologists have not fully considered native cultural definitions but have projected some supposed universal definitions of kinship on systems where they are inappropriate.

Cultures categorize kinsmen in numerous ways. Some cultures categorize lineal relatives with collaterals, while other cultures distinguish and differentiate these categories. Parallel cousins are sometimes grouped with siblings, and distinguished from cross-cousin categories. Some cultures reckon kinship according to matrilineal, patrilineal, or double unilineal descent systems. Some cultures categorize kinsmen by their place of residence or origin. Kinsmen are also categorized by such concepts as age, sex, and generation in many cultures. In some cultures, fathers or mothers may be categorized as relatives by marriage, instead of as relatives by substance. The various categories of kinsmen which exist in a particular culture constitute a major part of the cultural study of kinship.

Cultural systems structure the relationship between and among kinsmen and kin categories. In one culture, the relationship between father and child is strongly authoritarian; in other cultures, it may be warm and intimate, lacking in authority or discipline. In some cultures, the relationship between mother's brother and his sister's sons is like the relationship between mother and child; in other cultures, this relationship is structured in a way distinct from that between mother and child. Numerous examples of the way in which culture structures the relationships between and among kinsmen could be provided, but these will suffice for our purposes. The point here is simply that the way in which various kinship categories are linked together and the behavioral codes which outline these relationships are culturally defined and structured.

The cultural system explains the nature and meaning of kinship. This is an extremely important point for the study of kinship, even though it is not fully recognized by many scholars. Most studies of kinship have proceeded on the basis that the nature of kinship is the same for all cultures. This assumed universal nature of kinship is in fact taken from folk and scientific definitions of it in the Western world.

Marion Levy defines kinship as a structure developed by "an orientation to the facts of biological relatedness and/or sexual intercourse" (1952: 2). Meyer Fortes finds that "two facts" of life necessarily provide the basis of every family: the fact of sexual intercourse is institutionalized in marriage; the fact of parturition is institutionalized in parenthood (1959: 149). For Raymond Firth, "Kinship is fundamentally a reinterpretation in social terms of the facts of procreation and regularized sex union" (1936: 577).

The definitions of the nature of kinship listed above possess several common elements. First, they all presuppose the superiority of the epistemological system of modern science. Second, they assume that the scientifically defined facts of biological relatedness and sexual intercourse constitute the material out of which either social recognitions or cultural definitions are developed. Biology and sexual intercourse are the pie; kinship systems cut this pie in various ways, but it is that pie and no other that is being cut.

David Schneider has taken issue with this view of kinship. He argues:

> The reality of biology and/or sexual intercourse, then, does not have a single, simple, universal value which consists wholly and only in what can be scientifically established for it. It has a value in part related to its inherent qualities, but in part also fixed on what and on how it is culturally defined as meaningful, and on what part of all that is apprehended. The notion of a pure, pristine state of biological relationships "out there in reality" which is the same for all mankind is sheer nonsense. . . .
> If the assumption is that since kinship is merely the social

recognition and misapprehension of biological facts, then that assumption ought to be discarded since it is ridiculous. It is silly in part because the mere existence of a network of biological ties means nothing for the network of kinsmen by itself. (1965: 97–99.)

The point here is that there is no set of biological or sexual ties unless they are said by the culture to exist. The nature of these ties, if they exist, is culturally explained, and the meaning attributed to such ties is culturally derived and assigned. Each culture independently explains the nature and meaning of kinship.

Cultural systems relate the rules governing the moral order and organizational pattern of the kin universe. Kinship systems constitute coherent and patterned wholes, and are subject to structural analysis. Lévi-Strauss relates his methods of structural analysis to that used in structural linguistics. Such a structural analysis of kinship systems involves a distinction between statistical models and mechanical models (culture, for us), a treatment of the units of kinship not as independent entities but as related entities, and an overall focus on the concept of a system which bears structure (1963: 33, 283). Lévi-Strauss argues that in order to understand a concept such as the avunculate, it must be treated "as one relationship within a system, while the system itself must be considered as a whole in order to grasp its structure" (1963: 46).

The culturally related kin universe is a moral order because it is a statement of the proper order of that universe—that is, the ideal state of affairs or the way things ought to be. It refers to a condition in which everything is in its proper place, fulfilling its proper role and following all the cultural rules. The rules which govern the kin universe are moral rules. They state unconditionally how kinsmen behave toward each other and how groups of kinsmen function. They are axiomatic, based on a priori moral premises.

Kinship beliefs and attitudes are embodied in symbols. The symbols of kinship mean solidarity, and this solidarity is generally more intense, more diffuse, and more enduring than other kinds of solidarity (Schneider, 1968: 116). Although the symbols of kinship may be many and varied in a given culture, some of these symbols in all cultures are found in culturally defined processes of reproduction. The symbols provided by culturally defined processes of reproduction are of two basic types: actions involved in reproduction, or substances shared or transmitted through reproduction. Kinship solidarity may be distinguished from other forms of solidarity by the source of its symbols.

There is, however, no necessary relationship between reproduction and solidarity. Not only the actual processes but the nature as well of reproduction are culturally explained. This goes back to the earlier point that cultures explain the nature and meaning of the components of the universe. If the reproductive processes in a given culture have any meaning in terms of human solidarity, it is because the reproductive processes in that culture have been imbued by the culture with meaning related to human solidarity. In such a case, the reproductive processes would serve as symbols of kinship. If a culture did not imbue any of the reproductive processes with meaning in terms of solidarity, then such a culture would have no kinship system.

It is possible that, in a given culture, reproductive processes would be defined in such a way as to have little or no relationship to human solidarity. In such a culture, women might make children like they make pottery, and sell them for their value as laborers. The mother would in no way consider herself to be related by any form of solidarity to the children she makes. Such a cultural definition of motherhood would indeed be unusual, for all known cultures have imbued some of the reproductive processes with some kind of meaning in terms of solidarity. Yet this does not have to be so. The fact that it is so in all known cultures is a different matter altogether, but does merit some comment.

The actions and interactions involved in sexual intercourse and child birth forcefully lend themselves to be imbued with meaning in terms of human solidarity. The intense and powerful experiences of orgasm and the creation of a human being are vividly moving, and it seems natural that these experiences would be related to forms of human solidarity. In fact, this has been taken for granted because it seems so natural. Yet the fact that various cultures imbue different aspects of the reproductive process with great meaning in terms of solidarity, and others with little or no meaning, indicates that this meaning is culturally imbued and has no necessary relationship to any specific action or substance with regard to reproductive processes.

To summarize, kinship as a cultural system is a set of concepts, beliefs, and attitudes about solidarity which are embodied in symbols found in culturally defined reproductive processes. These symbols are imbued with powerful meaning that can generally be described as intense, diffuse, and enduring solidarity.

# 2  Mother and Child
## and the Nature of Kinship

The concepts of mother and child are inseparable in Navajo culture. To be a mother is to have a child—in the cultural sense, not in the biological sense. Fathers also have children, but the father-child relationship is distinctly different from the mother-child relationship. In order to define motherhood as a cultural construct, it is therefore necessary to define it in terms of the mother-child relationship.

Motherhood in Navajo culture is identified and defined in terms of life, particularly its source, reproduction, and sustenance. Mothers therefore give and sustain life for their children. The symbols of motherhood are based on the source, reproduction, and sustenance of life, and these symbols are imbued with powerful meanings in terms of solidarity. Mother and child are bound together by the most intense, the most diffuse, and the most enduring solidarity to be found in Navajo culture. Let us explore some of the specific symbols and meanings of motherhood.

The Navajo call Changing Woman, an important and central personality in Navajo mythology, by the term "-ma" (mother). The relationship of Changing Woman to her children provides the major conceptual framework for the Navajo cultural definition of motherhood.

At the time Changing Woman was found by First Man, the people had lost the ability to reproduce, and the monsters then inhabiting the world were killing the people. It was the plan of First Man, First Woman, and others to have Changing Woman restore the power of generation and to give birth to the Twins, who would destroy the monsters. At the time of Changing Woman's first menstrual period, the puberty rite was first performed for her. Haile's account explains the purpose of the ceremony:

Following these songs (hogan songs), all persons attending this ceremony contributed sets of songs, which purposed to again

bring man into being, and to enable him to give birth to his
kind. . . .

The songs used on that night were primarily for the benefit of
Changing Woman, with a view to enable her to create a new race,
and to transmit to this new race the power of generation.
(1938: 91, 251.)

After this ceremony, Changing Woman was united in conjugal
union with the Sun, and gave birth to the Twins and, later, the
original Navajo clans. In Navajo culture, life is created in, and
sustained by, mothers. Changing Woman was the source of life for
the "Dine" (Navajo), her children. She continues to sustain her
children today, for she is also symbolized by the earth. Earth Woman
is another one of her names (Reichard 1950: 431). Changing Woman
is so named because of her power repeatedly to reach old age and
then to return to youth. The power of the earth to go through its
seasons, rejuvenating each spring, is conceptually related to the
power of Changing Woman to return to her youth (Reichard 1950:
21).

Essential parts, as well as the earth itself, are called mother.
Agricultural fields are called mother, corn is called mother, and
sheep are called mother (Werner and Begishe 1968: 96, 105). These
applications of the concept -ma certainly make it clear that motherhood is defined in terms of the source, sustenance, and reproduction
of life. The Sun's decree concerning Whiteshell Woman (another
name of Changing Woman) further defines motherhood as a
cultural construct:

She will attend to her children and provide their food. Everywhere
I go over the earth she will have charge of female rain. I myself
will control male rain. She will be in control of vegetation everywhere for the benefit of Earth People. (Reichard 1950: 407.)

Earth Mother also provides the bond by which all living beings are
kindred (Franciscan Fathers, 1910: 35). All beings have their origin
in the underworlds and their existence on the earth's surface,
because in mythical times their progenitors emerged from previous
worlds below the earth's surface. The uterine bond between or
among siblings is expressed in the term "biɫhajiijeehigii" (those with
whom one came up out of the same womb).

The life and fertility of motherhood are symbolized not only by
the earth but also by corn pollen, yellow corn, and red menstrual

blood. According to one myth, Talking God gave corn to Whiteshell Woman and her sister Turquoise Woman, saying, "There is no better thing than this in the world, for it is the gift of life." Later, when Talking God visited them again and they told him they still had it, he said, "That is good, for corn is your symbol of fertility and life" (Reichard, 1950: 23).

Yellow corn is a symbol of female fertility, as the color yellow often is. In a study of Navajo symbolism, Newcomb, Fisher, and Wheelwright say:

> Yellow is the color of the female wind and of the ripened harvest and the soft autumn rain.... Yellow corn meal mush is the ceremonial food for the women as it indicates fertility, while white corn meal is prepared for the men. (1956: 15.)

Corn pollen, which is yellow, is probably the single most sacred item in the Navajo universe, and is a major symbol of female fertility. In order to give Changing Woman the power of generation, she was fed corn pollen (Spencer 1947: 56). Newcomb, Fisher, and Wheelwright say: "Pollen is the element which brings peace and plenty, long life, and security (1956: 38)." This certainly fits the source and subsistence of life meanings of motherhood symbols, and "security" suggests the affective meanings of motherhood.

The further association of the fertility of corn with human fertility is illustrated by the fact that the major symbolism of the Navajo wedding ceremony is the couple eating white corn (male) and yellow corn (female), both of which are mixed together with corn pollen sprinkled on top.

The fertility of motherhood is also symbolized by menstrual blood and the color red. Of all Navajo sex beliefs, the one which is most often mentioned and agreed upon is the danger of menstrual blood and the necessity of avoiding it. For Radcliffe-Brown, this avoidance would firmly establish the social value of menstrual blood (1952: 141-43). This analysis is probably correct if we add that it is not the substance of the symbol (the blood itself) which is valued but the meaning of the symbol—the fertility of human mothers.

The fact that menstrual blood is a symbol of human fertility is further suggested by the belief that sexual intercourse with a menstruating woman insures conception. Additional verification can be found in the Navajo belief that conception occurs by the combination of the man's water (semen) and the woman's blood (menstrual). Bailey's informant stated this belief clearly:

The blood (menstrual) that doesn't come turns into the baby (evidenced by the fact that the women cease menstruation at conception). Water from a man and (menstrual) blood from a woman make the baby. (1950: 18.)

The "redness" of menstrual blood is used in other places as a life and fertility symbol. Newcomb says,

Red occupies an important place in the color symbolism of all Navajo sand paintings, as it represents the life principle of animals as well as immortals. (1956: 16.)

It is also not insignificant or accidental that the belt suspended from the roof of the hogan to which the mother holds in labor during childbirth is red. The association of the fertility of corn and that of human mothers is verified when the singer in charge sprinkles corn pollen on the red belt of the delivering mother (Bailey 1950: 56-57).

In the puberty rite, the fertility of the earth, the corn, and the girl for whom the ceremony is performed are all symbolized by the cake made of corn. A red mixture called "chii dik'ǫsh" (red ocher and red sumac) is mixed with the corn, symbolizing the girl's menstrual blood and fertility. The cake is placed in the earth. On the last morning of the ceremony, the cake is brought "up out" of the earth. All this goes back in myth to Changing Woman's reproductive role and symbols.

The myth connected to the puberty rite explains some of the meanings of the cake:

She also told the people to make a round cake, representing Mother Earth during the Kinaaldá....

After she had done these things, anyone who wanted to was allowed to take a pinch of corn meal and do what she had done, while praying for good luck, plenty, good vegetation, and no hunger, hardships, or suffering ... (Frisbie 1967: 12, 14).

Motherhood and Changing Woman are also associated with the mountain soil bundle. In discussing the mountain soil bundle, Wyman makes the following comment:

To an individual it is his "medicine," the source of blessings, like the magic bundle of First Man. It can produce things, the comforts of life, absence of worry, accumulation of property, insuring a long and happy life.... He speaks of it as "our mother" because Changing Woman and her Blessingway gave it to us. (1970: 22.)

In a recent study of the Navajo puberty rite, Charlotte Frisbie comments on the many connected symbols of the rite:

> In the Kinaaldá, the girl herself is a symbol, not only of the major Navajo diety, Changing Woman (and her counterparty, White Shell Woman, Turquoise Woman, and others) and the concepts with which she is associated, such as Earth and Life, but also of the power of reproduction. Her coming of age is connected with new growth of plants and changes in environmental conditions. ... The food used in Kinaaldá also has symbolic meaning. Corn, the symbol of food, fertility, and life itself, is of major importance. "Corn is more than human; it is divine...." (Reichard 1950: 540.)
> The pollen applied in order to attain blessing represents control. It is an outstanding "symbol of life and protection, fructification, verification, and the continuity of life and safety" (Reichard 1950: 250). (Frisbie 1967: 373-76.)

Changing Woman's relationship to her children was also focused on subsistence:

> She was extremely kind to her children, promised them variegated corn, seeds, and plants of all kinds, medicines in case of sickness, precious stones (ntl'is), and all her protection in general. Therefore, all good things, the mild rains, the growth of corn, etc., all are due to her beneficient influence, and come from the West. (Franciscan Fathers 1910: 356.)

The personality of Changing Woman and her objective representation, the earth, closely embody the cultural definitions and meanings of motherhood. Gladys Reichard, whom I consider to be the anthropologist who learned Navajo culture best, gives her appraisal of Changing Woman:

> Changing Woman is the most fascinating of the many appealing characters conjured up by the Navajo imagination.... Changing Woman is Woman with a sphinx like quality. She is the mystery of reproduction, of life springing from nothing, of the last hope of the world, a riddle perpetually solved and perennially springing up anew, literally expressed in Navajo: "... here the one who is named Changing Woman, the one who is named Whiteshell Woman, here her name is pretty close to the (real) names of every one of the girls."
> Changing Woman's power over reproduction and birth extends to all that exists on the earth.... Many of Changing Woman's

gifts are rites or ceremonies, not fully enumerated here. Her decrees are kind.... She was present at Rainboy's chant, and at another time brought in ceremonial food. Her presence at an assembly of the gods is pointed out with respect. Other gods bow their heads when she comes in. (1950: 407, 413.)

From the preceding analysis of the personality of Changing Woman, her symbols, and her relationship to her children, the definitions and meanings of motherhood become clear. A mother is one who gives life through birth to her children, and then sustains the life of her children by giving them both physical and emotional sustenance. The acts of giving birth and sustenance are imbued with meaning from the cultural system, and this meaning can be described as intense, diffuse, and enduring solidarity.

According to these cultural concepts and definitions, the Navajo refer to the earth as "nihima" (our mother). Such references to kinship with the earth have previously been categorized as metaphorical. I believe that this reference to the earth as our mother is based on more than simply a metaphorical extension of the concepts of kinship. In Navajo mythology, the earth was the source of life for all beings through their emergence from the underworlds. In this act of emergence, the earth gave birth to all living creatures. The earth continues to sustain the life of her children by providing them with food and other forms of protection and sustenance. The emotional or affective tie between the Navajo and the earth is also strong and intense. Thus by every Navajo cultural concept and definition, the earth is a mother, a true kinswoman.

In an excellent treatment of the "Symbolic Elements in Navajo Ritual," Louise Lamphere comes to some interesting conclusions:

Navajo ritual identification and removal imply an alternative to Turner's analysis of Ndembu symbols, where concepts derived from bodily experiences are projected onto the natural and social world. In Navajo chants, natural products are transformed into objects associated with the supernaturals, and these in turn are applied to or taken into the body; disease-causing elements which are simultaneously supernatural and natural are expelled. Rather than body processes being relevant to classifying the world, concepts concerning the natural-supernatural world are relevant to interpreting body processes. (1969: 279.)

If "concepts concerning the natural-supernatural world are relevant to interpreting body processes," then is it possible that the concept of the earth and her relationship to her children is relevant to interpreting body processes such as giving birth and nourishment? Maybe it is the earth who is really mother, and human mothers merely resemble the earth in some ways and are not really mothers.

Mircea Eliade, looking at this matter of Mother Earth from a different perspective, came to a similar conclusion:

> This fundamental experience—that the human mother is only the representative of the tellurice Great Mother—has given rise to countless customs. . . .
>
> The religious meaning of the custom is easy to see: generation and childbirth are microcosmic versions of a paradigmatic act performed by the earth; every human mother only imitates and repeats this primordial act of the appearance of life in the womb of the earth. (1959: 142.)

This is mentioned only to suggest that a strong argument could be made for the earth being the primary referent or denotatum of the term "-ma." Nevertheless, the Navajo claim both the earth and human mothers as mothers, and a cultural analysis of Navajo kinship should follow Navajo cultural definitions.

For those who follow American and European cultural beliefs, according to which "real" or "true" kinship is limited to those human beings who are blood relatives, it must be pointed out that Navajo define kinship in terms of action or behavior, not in terms of substance.

Although the Navajo believe that through sexual intercourse and birth some kind of common substance is shared (Bailey 1950: 18), their culture attaches no meaning to this alleged common substance. The Navajo never mention common substance in finding or invoking kinship ties and norms. Kinship is discussed in terms of the acts of giving birth and sharing sustenance.

The primary bond in the Navajo kinship system is the mother-child bond, and it is in this bond that the nature and meaning of kinship become clear. In Navajo culture, kinship means intense, diffuse, and enduring solidarity, and this solidarity is realized in actions and behavior befitting the cultural definitions of kinship solidarity. Just as a mother is one who gives life to her children through birth, and sustains their life by providing them with loving care, assistance, protection, and sustenance, kinsmen are those who sustain each other's life by helping one another, protecting one another, and by the giving or sharing of food and other items of subsistence. Where this kind of solidarity exists, kinship exists; where it does not exist, there is no kinship.

# 3 Marriage and the Nature of Affinity

In Navajo culture, kinship is distinct from, but juxtaposed to, affinity. Kinship solidarity is framed and focused in the concepts of sharing and giving. Nonkinship solidarity is framed in systems of exchange and reciprocity. One of the major forms of nonkinship solidarity is that of marriage and affinal relations derived from marriage. Whereas kinsmen must not copulate, the primary symbol of affinal solidarity is found in sexual intercourse.

Sexual intercourse necessarily involves male and female entities. One of the major aspects of the preemergence period was the attempt to work out a proper relationship between the sexes. Reichard describes these events as follows:

> Sexual indulgence was a preoccupation of the inhabitants of the lower worlds; it led to the floods which necessitated the emergence. First Man taunted his wife with being interested in sex alone. His rebuke gave rise to a quarrel in which she said that women could get along without men. To prove the challenge the men moved across the river and destroyed the rafts that had carried them. As years went by, the women became weaker; they needed the men's strength to produce food, and they became maddened with desire. As a result of self-abuse they gave birth to the monsters that later destroyed men. The men too practiced perversion, but from their excesses no evil survived. After many had died and great suffering had ensued, the women yielded and begged the men to take them back. They did so, and all agreed that henceforth man should be the leader in matters of sex since he belonged to the stronger sex. (1950: 31.)

These mythological events dramatize the necessity of a proper union between males and females as a basis for satisfactory reproduction. The men by themselves could not have children, and the women by themselves could produce only monsters. Another reproductive symbol—food—could not be produced effectively without male assistance. Only in proper relations with men could women effectively and satisfactorily produce children and food.

When First Man and First Woman were fumbling with creation, including institutions and practices as well as things, First Woman created

> ... male and female genitalia so that one sex should attract the other—the penis of turquoise, the vagina of white shell. After treating them ritualistically, she laid them side by side and blew over them medicine (infusion), which was to cause pregnancy. She went further and determined the degree of desire—great for men, much less for women. Intercourse was to leave the penis weak, the vagina strong. (Reichard 1950: 31.)

The implication is that only by the pairing of males and females can reproduction take place. The fact that conception and reproduction take place through the union of male and female symbols is further verified by the Navajo belief that the man's water (semen) and woman's blood (menstrual) make the baby (Bailey 1950: 18).

Male and female are basic symbols. Numerous components of the Navajo universe are in binary opposition to each other through male and female forms: east/west, blue/red, white (corn)/yellow (corn), sun/earth, sky/ground, light/darkness, hard rain/soft rain, forked hogan/round hogan, water (semen)/blood (menstrual), turquoise shell/white shell, and a multitude of male and female plants, mountains, and ceremonies.

Through their distinctiveness, males and females are related to each other as complementary equals. Specifically, this means relations of exchange and reciprocity. In Navajo society, a woman bestows sexual favors on a man in exchange for something of economic value. It is wrong to copulate with a man without receiving something of value from him.

The most obvious form in which a man exchanges items of value (economic power) for sexual favors (reproductive power) is found in bridewealth. That this exchange is for reproductive power is suggested by the fact that if a wife proves unable to bear children, her husband may—and usually does—leave her and ask for the bridewealth to be returned. Even when marriage occurs without a ceremony, bridewealth is expected and usually provided. The bridewealth makes the marital relationship proper and complete. If the bridewealth is not provided, the man is accused of theft.

Informal sexual relations, whether premarital or extramarital, are also properly realized in similar forms of exchange. In the autobiography *Son of Old Man Hat*, gifts in exchange for informal sexual relations are mentioned several times (Dyk 1938: 212, 288, 344). Ladd also mentions this phenomenon:

> There are many other ways in which sex is assimilated to property.
> Illicit sexual intercourse is "just like stealing." There is an
> ancient practice of paying a woman with whom one has had
> sexual intercourse. Moreover, if a woman takes a piece of
> property she wants to be seduced, and if she has been seduced, she
> appropriates a piece of the man's property. There are numerous
> other practices which illustrate the same close relationship be-
> tween sex and property; for example, the bride price custom and
> the custom of paying women partners at squaw dances. (Ladd,
> 1957: 210-11.)

Although this is a good summary of the data on exchange and sexual relations, its main point is not necessarily correct, because the exchange of a commodity for sexual favors does not make sex a commodity any more than it makes the commodity sex. We should also be careful not to impose our concepts of sexual morality on the Navajo. The exchange of something for sexual favors is not considered prostitution. On the contrary, sexual relations without exchange are considered immoral.

Marriage in Navajo society is defined in terms of cohabitation (ahiɬ sike) and sexual intercourse. The concept of marriage is thus symbolized in the concrete acts of cohabitation and sexual intercourse. Sexual partners who do not live together can be considered to be married by the fact that the acts of sexual intercourse and exchange correspond to one side of the dual defining features of marriage. On the other hand, if the defining feature of sexual intercourse is ignored, sexual partners who do not live together can be considered not married. This is interestingly demonstrated in a set of events in the life of the Son of Old Man Hat (Dyk 1938: 342-44).

The reciprocal nature of the affinal bond is demonstrated in the following marriage proposal:

> As soon as I said, "I want my son to marry your daughter," they
> said, "We do too. We want our daughter to marry your son."
> I stayed there, and we talked about things, and I told them you

had lots of work to do at home. "You know he's all alone, just with his mother, and they both need help. So now we'll all help each other. You help us, and we'll help you." After that I said, "My son and I will give you twelve horses." (Dyk 1938: 370–71.)

This example strongly suggests that marriage involves a reciprocal arrangement of affinal solidarity between the relatives of the marrying individuals as well as between the marrying individuals themselves.

There are two major kinds of affinal solidarity in Navajo culture. One is marital ties, and the other consists in the affinal ties derived from marriage. These derived affinal ties exist in varying degrees, depending upon the relative distance of a particular kinsman to the spouse through whom the affinal tie is realized. For example, the category in the closest affinal position (other than his wife) to a man is his wife's mother, next is her sister, and third is her brother. This is because his wife is closest to her mother, second closest to her sister, and third closest to her brother.

Because the affinal bond is symbolized by sexual intercourse, the obvious and logical objects of a man's sexual expressions of affinity beyond his wife are, first, his wife's mother and, second, his wife's sisters. However, his wife's mother is sexually forbidden to him. Specifically, the rule says the son-in-law must not look upon his mother-in-law. In fact, the son-in-law refers to his mother-in-law as "doo yish'iinii" ("the one whom I do not see").

Communication with one's eyes is related to romantic enticements and seductions. Sexual desire is, in part, communicated through one's eyes. A mother-in-law is sexually taboo, and therefore should not be looked upon by the eyes of a son-in-law. Ethnographers have said the Navajo have a rule of mother-in-law avoidance, but in cultural terms this avoidance is mainly sexual avoidance. A son-in-law may talk to his mother-in-law, help her, and sometimes even touch her through shaking hands, so long as he does not look at her.

Though the one in the closest affinal position to a son-in-law is sexually taboo to him, those in the second position of affinal closeness, wife's sisters, are not necessarily taboo for him. They are taboo for him if they are already married, according to the rules of adultery. If they are not married, they are prime objects of extra-marital sexual relations. Men who have more than one wife usually marry sisters. The Franciscans report on this:

To obviate dissension and to insure conjugal fidelity recourse is had to marriage with the sisters of one's wife, a course which is favorably viewed by the wife's parents if the son-in-law proves industrious and decent otherwise. In this event, however, the marriage ceremony may not take place, but the second and third wives are added to the first without ceremony (banaholtge, she is given to him in addition to the other, a wife's sister). . . . The so-called ch' aena'l, or privilege of marrying the sister of a deceased wife, was also conceded to the widow in regard to the brothers of her late husband, and many are still faithful to this custom. (1910: 449.)

The lack of a need for a wedding ceremony and bridewealth in the situations mentioned above suggests that affinal bonds have already been established through the initial marriage. Rules of mother-in-law avoidance and adultery prohibitions limit the sexual realizations of these derived affinal bonds. Sexual intercourse is, however, not the only way in which affinal ties are expressed and realized; mutual cooperation, economic reciprocity, and all kinds of exchange are other ways in which affinal bonds are expressed and realized.

As shown in chapter 2, the primary bond of kinship in Navajo culture exists between mother and child. The primary affinal bond exists between husband and wife. Other kinship and affinal ties are secondary or more distant because they are linked by one or more intermediary persons or categories. A man relates in a primary way to two women during his lifetime, his mother and his wife (assuming he marries). A woman has a primary relationship with one other woman, her mother, and one man, her husband (assuming she marries), in addition to her children.

A Navajo man is virtually tossed between two women, and through them he gets his status and works out his role in the social system. His relationship to these two women involves two kinds of relationship to a womb. One is a kind of extrusion; the other is a kind of intrusion. One is symbolized by birth; the other, by sexual intercourse. One is described as the utmost in security; the other is considered to hold latent danger. One involves sharing; the other, exchange. One involves cognatic solidarity; the other, conjugal solidarity. As a youth, Son of Old Man Hat was concerned about this other woman matter:

Once I asked my mother, "What relation is my father to you?

What relation do you call him: I call you my mother, and I call my father my father. What do you call my father, and what does he call you? How are you related to each other?" When I said this to her she said, "He's my husband." She said it in a loud voice, and she scared me with what she said. She said, "A man and woman who are together like that are husband and wife. The man is husband to the woman, and the woman is wife to the man. That's why they call each other my husband and my wife. You'll be that way when you grow up to be a man. You'll have a wife just like these men now." I said, "I don't want to go near a woman who's not related to me, because she's not my mother." She said, "You don't know anything about it yet, because you're small. When you grow up to be a man, you'll get a woman and when she wants to leave you you'll be hanging onto her, even though she's not your mother. You'll be hanging on to her ... just as if she were your mother. ..."

"It's pretty dangerous to have a wife or a husband...."
(Dyk 1938: 47–48.)

To summarize, affinity in Navajo culture is in complementary opposition to kinship. These involve two kinds of primary relationships to a woman who stands in the position of a wife to one and a mother to the other. Affinal solidarity involves the concepts of exchange and reciprocity, and the primary symbols of affinal solidarity are found in the cohabitation and sexual intercourse features of the marriage relationship. Kinship solidarity involves sharing or giving, and the primary bond of kinship is symbolized in the acts of bearing and rearing which define the mother-child relationship. The mother-child relationship is strong and secure, while the husband-wife relationship is often weak and insecure. In any case, they provide the primary building blocks of the Navajo system of social solidarity.

# 4    Father and Child

In chapters 2 and 3, the contrasting but complementary forms of kinship and affinal solidarity were discussed and described. The father-child relationship will now be analyzed in the light of these two forms of solidarity. Since the monumental work of Lewis Henry Morgan, *Systems of Consanguinity and Affinity of the Human Family*, affinity and consanguinity have been considered as opposite kinds of relationship which could not occur in the same relationship. Therefore the Navajo father must be related to his children by either kinship or affinity. Meyer Fortes argues that in a unilineal descent system a child is normally related to the parent who does not determine descent by complementary filiation, a form of kinship.

Complementary filiation is a term developed by Fortes to explain the usual relationship of an inmarrying affine to his or her children who belong to a unilineal core. The concept is related to Fortes' view of the nature and function of lineage systems in homogeneous societies. Fortes says, "The most important feature of unilineal descent groups in Africa ... is their corporate organization" (1953: 25). With the lineage being a corporation and with recruitment restricted to unilineal descent, the inmarrying affine is in a peculiar position with regard to his children. Fortes characterizes this relationship as complementary filiation.

Fortes states that filiation is, in contrast to descent, universally bilateral. For him, the bilateral nature of filiation is recognized by the lineage group and utilized for purposes of segmenting society, linking sibling groups, building double unilineal systems, and differentiating various aspects of inheritance and succession (1953: 33–35).

Leach has discussed the dissatisfaction of alliance theorists with Fortes' concept of complementary filiation:

The structural ties deriving from marriage between members of different corporations have been largely ignored or else assimilated into the all-important descent concept. Thus Fortes (1953), while recognizing that ties of affinity have comparable importance to ties of descent, disguises the former under his expression "complementary filiation." . . . For Fortes, marriage ties, as such, do not form part of the structural system. (1961: 122.)

Leach pursues his point of view even further, and says that the Trobriand father is related to his children by affinity, not by filiation.[1] He also provides supporting data that the converse is possible:

> Of what sort of society could we say that a child is unrelated to its mother—in the sense that there is no bond of social filiation between mother and child? Clearly the converse of the Trobriand argument applies. If there is a society in which the relation between a child and its mother is utterly unlike that between a child and its father but has much in common with the relations between cross-cousins and between brothers-in-law, then this mother/child relationship is not sensibly described as one of filiation. It is rather a relationship of affinity traced through the father. (1961: 13.)

Let us now explore the Navajo ethnography to see whether there is any reason to suspect that the Navajo father-child relationship might be best characterized by affinity. There are a number of aspects of the Navajo ethnography which would lead one to the conclusion that this relationship is characterized by affinity.

First, as I showed in another paper (1970) and as Aberle's work verifies, the intensity or closeness of the father-child relationship varies proportionally to the intensity or closeness of the father-mother relationship:

> There is a high rate of divorce. There are a fair number of cases in which a woman dies young, her children remain with her kin, and their father remarries elsewhere. Hence ties between father and children are weakened. There is no traditional claim of children on their father for property or support after a divorce, and a divorced man may maintain little interest in his children. In cases where the marriage is stable, the relationship can be described as intense (affectionate and intimate) but not strong; it does not compete successfully with the mother's claims in case of divorce, or with the bonds to a man's natal family. (1961: 167.)

In other words, from a behavioral or functional point of view, it is the marriage of the father to the mother which ties the father to his children. When the marriage is dissolved, the father-child relationship is behaviorally and functionally dissolved, or almost so.

Second, Navajo children often refer to and address their father as an in-law. The term "shaadaani" ("male-in-law of a proximate generation") is often used in a joking context by a Navajo child in addressing or referring to his father. I have personally observed this practice a number of times, and Aberle's informant stated the same thing (1961: 152).

Third, marriage practices among the Navajo tend to indicate that father's clansmen are thought of as ideal affinal relatives. Some Navajo say it is good to marry into one's father's clan. Reichard lists marriage into one's father's clan as a major marriage preference (1928: 65).

The practice of Navajo men marrying a woman with children and then also marrying the woman's oldest daughter is well documented. Reichard elaborates further:

> The gift of the daughter is not necessarily restricted to a time when the mother is too old to bear children for there was one case where a man had married mother and daughter. The daughter was holding a baby not more than a year old who was said to be her "sister." It was really the daughter of the girl's mother and of the husband of both of them. (1928: 62–63.)

Reichard reports another interesting marriage in this regard. In this case, a woman (A) married a man (B), and they had two daughters (A_1 and A_2). This marriage was later dissolved. Then the original husband's mother's brother (B_1) married the woman (A) and, later, her two daughters (A_1 and A_2) (Reichard, 1928: 63).

Spencer's *Reflection of Social Life in the Navaho Origin Myth* shows no prohibition against marriage into the father's clan:

> The only marriage regulations mentioned are those prohibiting marriage between brothers and sisters (MD70, 137), and marriage with a person of one's own clan (G 128). (1947: 33.)

This accords with statements of one of my best informants, who said that no prohibition against marriage into the father's clan existed in the preemergence and early postemergence periods.

Much of Navajo mythology seems to focus on the concept of father-daughter marriage. Spencer summarizes:

The relatively complicated series of events compromising these witch father-in-law episodes occur with great stability and frequency (Plume, Navaho Wind, Chiricahua Wind, Eagle, Shooting-Ghostway). The episode opens when the hero discovers a family living apart, consisting of father, mother and daughter. The visitor is immediately greeted as a son-in-law, but in offering this apparent welcome the father acts deceitfully and secretly plots the hero's destruction. The reason for the father's malevolence is sometimes explicitly stated. ... He is married not only to his proper wife but also to his daughter; he is thus jealous of the new son-in-law. (1957: 28–29.)

The myths continue by having the father-in-law plot the son-in-law's destruction, but the hero is able to circumvent all attempts on his life and to compel his father-in-law to confess that he is a witch.

One can interpret these mythological events in many ways. Certainly one interpretation would be that the father is related to his daughter by affinity, and thus might have erotic interest in her. Such marriages would, however, severely limit the recruitment of much-needed sons-in-law. Therefore father-daughter marriage is prohibited.

Although the Navajo descent system will be discussed in a separate chapter, a simple logical explanation of why a Navajo is related to his father's clan by affinity will be briefly mentioned here. Ego is assigned to his mother's matrilineal descent category, and ego's father is related to this category by affinity; therefore, by virtue of the fact that ego has the same descent identity as his mother, ego is related to his father by affinity. This does not mean, however, that this is the only way in which ego is related to his father.

If the Navajo father is related to his child by affinity, is it also possible that he could be related to his child by filiation?

There are many ethnographic data which suggest a relationship of filiation between father and child in Navajo culture and society. A simple example which seems to contradict the affinity concept is that the Navajo term "sha'aℓchini" (my child or my children) can be used by either a father or a mother. The use of this term by a father with regard to his children is continued after the termination of a father's marriage to the mother of his children. In some cases, a father and his matrilineal relatives may take the children after the marriage is terminated (Reichard 1928: 55). In general, the relationship of a father to his children is one of affection, discipline, instruction, and economic assistance. This would have to be described as complementary to the mother-child bond, although it is not as close, intense, and permanent as the mother-child bond.

One response to contradictory data in Navajo ethnography has been to state that Navajo culture and social organization are truly fuzzy or flexible and to explain this genuine flexibility in terms of some variables such as Aberle has articulated (1963: 1–8). Anthropologists studying the Navajo might also consider the possibility that the data are not contradictory, but their understanding of them is less than adequate. The fuzziness might exist more in the minds of anthropologists than in Navajo culture. As I have stated previously, I am not convinced that Navajo culture is as fuzzy as some think. Part of the problem may well be due to the ethnographer's failure to fully understand Navajo cultural categories.

Just as Navajo refer to Changing Woman as "nihima" ("our mother"), they refer to the Sun as "nihitah" ("our father"). The Sun and his associated symbols and their meanings provide the major conceptual framework for the Navajo cultural definition of fatherhood. The Sun is actually considered a being with human form and characteristics, but one who is closely identified with the sun, his objective symbol (Reichard 1950: 18).

The Sun's relationship to his children in mythology is one of distance and assistance. This distance is conceptualized both in his relationship to his children in mythology and in the distance of his objective symbol, the sun, from the earth, which is the habitation of his children. In contrast, the closeness of a mother to her children is conceptualized by Changing Woman's closeness to her children in mythology and in the closeness of her objective symbol, the earth, to her children.

The Sun, a source of protective assistance, is also unmerciful and sometimes destructive to his children. He forced the Twins to go through rigorous trials and tests before giving them his attention and assistance. He then provided the Twins with the weapons and charms necessary to exercise power over their enemies. He also instructed the Twins in the use of the weapons, charms, and many other things. At the time he was helping the Twins, he was taking part in the destruction of one of his own children, for one of the giants was a child of the Sun. On several other occasions the Sun took harmful action toward his children, ignored their desires and needs, and sometimes took the side of some of his children against others of his children. So, at best, a father is a helpful friend, a good teacher, and a strong disciplinarian; at worst, he is a potential enemy, an undependable friend, or an unreliable ally. In any case, a father has much affection for, and interest in, his children, for the Sun wept and suffered when he helped the Twins destroy one of the giants who was also his child (Spencer 1947: 44).

Katherine Spencer, in *Mythology and Values*, presents a lengthy discussion of the conflicting attitudes toward fathers in both Navajo mythology and ethnography. She concludes that the Navajo father has a "double image" or a "double conception" (1947: 67). She states that projective tests given to Navajo youth reflect this double image of fathers.

My own explanation of this dual relationship between fathers and their children has become obvious by now—that the Navajo father is related to his children by both kinship and affinity. This duality of relationship comes directly out of the Navajo view of the reproductive process, and is supported by all the data mentioned here and much more which could have been mentioned. The structure of the relationships discussed in chapters 2, 3, and 4 can be diagramed as in figure 1.

Figure 1. Structure of relationships in nuclear family

This structure involves two primary bonds. One is the conjugal bond between husband and wife, or father and mother. The other is the uterine bond between mother and child. Both of these bonds involve relationships to the same womb, but each relationship is of a different kind. One is a kind of intrusion, symbolized by sexual intercourse. The other is a kind of extrusion, symbolized by birth. One is defined as the utmost in security and solidarity (chapter 2); the other is considered fragile, containing latent danger (chapter 3).

One involves solidarity symbolized by sharing; the other, solidarity symbolized by exchange.

Along with the husband-wife and the mother-child relationships in the Navajo kinship structure, there are the father-child and sibling-sibling relationships. These relationships are not primary relationships in the sense that the husband-wife and mother-child relationships are primary. The father-child and sibling-sibling relationships are traced through, and linked together by, another category, the mother. From another perspective, the line initiated by the husband (father) into the mother's womb is continued out of the womb to the children (Wyman 1970: 349–50). This link involves both an affinal and a consanguinal relationship. The father-child relationship involves both a strong bond (kinship) and a weak bond (affinity), depending on perspective and emphasis. This dual relationship corresponds with the earlier definition of the father-child relationship, where the father was defined as a somewhat distant relative who was, at best, a helpful friend, good instructor, and strong disciplinarian, or, at worst, an undependable friend, inconsistent helper, or unsure ally.

The other major relationship in this elementary kinship structure is that between siblings. Again, the mother's womb provides the connecting link. The two lines of kinship connected at the womb are both consanguinal, uterine bonds. They are both strong and second only in strength to those between mother and child, for they are of the same type. This uterine bond among siblings is expressed in the term "bił hajiijeehigii" ("those with whom one came up out of the same womb").

The Navajo father relates to his children in a way similar to that of a mother and that of an affine.[2] Seen in the light of this dual relationship, the contradictory data presented here become comprehensible. Normally in social relations, the stronger bond, the one of kinship, is emphasized, but the culturally defined link of affinity is always there and may be invoked in certain social contexts.

Probably an even more significant point which has slowly been emerging through these initial chapters is the fact that all ties (affinal and consanguinal) have as one of their defining features the mother's womb as a focal point, and are symbolized in different kinds of action—birth and sexual intercourse—with regard to the mother's womb. At the end of chapter 3, it was shown that a Navajo man is literally tossed between two women, his mother and his wife.

In the autobiography *Son of Old Man Hat*, the transition from one to the other is described as difficult and dangerous, though a Navajo never completely severs his tie with his mother. She is always there in case of trouble.

# 5    The Descent System

The Navajo term "k'e" means "compassion," "cooperation," "friendliness," "unselfishness," "peacefulness," and all those positive virtues which constitute intense, diffuse, and enduring solidarity. The term "k'ei" means "a special or particular kind of k'e." It is this term (k'ei) which is used to signify the system of descent relationships and categories found in Navajo culture. "Shik'ei" ("my relatives by descent") distinguishes a group of relatives with whom one relates according to a special kind of k'e.

Before I discuss the Navajo system of descent in detail, it may be helpful to clarify some conceptual and terminological conventions which are commonly used by anthropologists in discussing descent systems but which may be used somewhat differently here.

In studying and discussing descent systems, there are three important aspects which must be distinguished and differentiated: descent relationship, descent category, and descent group. A descent category exists on the cultural level, while a descent group exists on the social level. By "category," I mean a set of conceptually defined elements which fall together only in the sense that they share a common element. By "group," I mean an aggregate of real persons which may make decisions, take collective action, and/or hold property.

Both descent categories and descent groups are based on descent relationships, but descent relationships may also exist independent of either descent categories or descent groups. For example, if in a particular culture a child is defined as a descendant of its father, a relationship of descent may be said to exist between the father and the child. This descent relationship is not necessarily utilized in the formulation of a descent category. A descent category involves a set of descent relationships which are defined as the same and categorized together. Where a number of persons share the same father-child relationship, they constitute a descent category.

Where those of the same descent category also constitute a social group, where they act as a group, perhaps come together to reach decisions or dispose of assets, they constitute a descent group. Where a descent category is not utilized in the formation of a descent group, it may be given other meanings in the social system.

A descent relationship, a descent category, and a descent group may be three aspects of the same thing, but not always. It is therefore important to distinguish between them and to show how they are related to each other.

A descent relationship must come first, for the other two are both based on it. A descent category comes second, and is based on the first, a descent relationship. A descent group comes third, because a descent group must be based on, first, a descent relationship and, second, a descent category. In other words, the first (descent relationship) may exist without the second (descent category) and the third (descent group); the second can exist only with the first, but may exist with or without the third; the third can exist only with the first and the second.

What I have called a "descent relationship" is similar to what Fortes has called "filiation." His concept of "complementary filiation" is simply where a descent relationship is not the basis for a unilineal descent group but where another is. It seems to me that Fortes has, however, failed to give full consideration to descent categories where they are not the bases of descent groups.

Among the Navajo, the descent relationship which Fortes calls "complementary" is used by the culture as a basis for formulating one or more descent categories. These descent categories are not, however, unilineal, and do not have social counterparts which can be called descent groups. They are, nevertheless, important in ordering behavior and social relationships, as we shall see later in this chapter. Because, it seems to me, insufficient attention has been given to descent categories, a brief discussion of the many possible descent categories will be provided here.

As Radcliffe-Brown (Radcliffe-Brown and Forde 1950: 13) indicates, descent relationships consist of two basic kinds: one is descended from the other, or they both are descended from a common ancestor. Where descent is bilateral, a child is recognized as a descendent of both father and mother. This extends on to maternal and paternal grandparents and beyond them. The latter kind of descent exists between siblings who have the same father or mother or both. These two basic kinds of descent relationships are used by cultural systems to formulate and define various kinds of descent categories.

The first and best known is the unilineal descent category. In a matrilineal descent system, the mother-child relationship is abstracted from the genealogical network and used to define matrilineal descent categories. In such a system, the child is given the same descent identity as its mother. The children of all the women of the category stay in that category, while children of the men are not included because the father-child relationship of descent is not the one on which the category is based. The result is a system wherein the descent category is also an inclusive category—that is, it includes both units of a descent relationship, mother and child, in the same descent category.

Lineal descent categories are not confined only to unilineal systems. Descent categories may be bilineal. The Daughters of the American Revolution is a bilineal descent category. The descendants of Abraham Lincoln may be defined as a bilineal descent category.

Studies of descent categories and groups do not have to be limited to systems having lineal descent categories and groups. Non-lineal or exclusive descent categories[1] are those in which a child's descent identity comes from one of its relatives by descent, such as its mother, but is different from the descent identity of its mother. For example, a mother is in category A, but all her children are in category B. In fact, all the children of the women of category A are assigned to category B. Category B is thus defined as all the children of the women of category A. In such a system, the child inherits descent identity from its mother, but this descent identity is not the same as that of its mother's. The children of descent category B may be identified as A or may be something entirely different. This kind of a descent category is not lineal and is exclusive, which means that the child inherits an identity from its parent but that the identity excludes the parent.

Nonlineal descent categories may skip a link or generation. In such a case, a child may inherit descent identity from one of his grandparents. This kind of descent category may be inclusive or exclusive. If a child's paternal grandmother is A and the child inherits this same A identity and passes it on to its paternal grandchildren, the category is inclusive. If, however, the category is made up of all those whose paternal grandmothers are A but does not include their paternal grandmothers, the category is something other than A and is exclusive of one of the units in the abstracted relationship.

Lineal and nonlineal, inclusive and exclusive, and unilineal and bilineal descent categories are not mutually exclusive, but may coincide in the same kinship system. Nonlineal descent categories often coincide with, and are complementary to, unilineal descent categories. Having defined and differentiated the concepts of descent relationship, descent category, and descent group, and having outlined many of the possible kinds of descent categories, I shall now proceed to an analysis of the Navajo descent system.

The Navajo system has two basic kinds of descent categories: unilineal and nonlineal, or inclusive and exclusive. An individual Navajo may, however, be related to as many as sixty different descent categories.

The first and probably the most important categories in the Navajo descent system are the matrilineal descent categories. Navajo mythology relates that matrilineal descent categories had their origin in the creations of Changing Woman:

> Among the clans four claim the distinction of originating directly from the person of "esdzanadle," the Changing Woman. The "kiiya'ani" were created from the skin which she removed from her breast, wherefore their name is said to signify "those made of her breast." In like manner, the "honaghani," or "they who were made of her back," were created from the skin which she loosened from her back, while the "tqadich'ini," bitter water people, and the "tquotsoni" big water people, are so called because of their creation from the sweat (or skin) gathered from below her right and left arm respectively. (Franciscan Fathers 1910: 427.)

Since the mythical time, when there were just four matrilineal descent categories, about sixty more have come into existence. Various legends relate the origins of these clans (Sapir and Hoijer 1942: 80-97). These approximately sixty matrilineal categories are grouped together into nine main categories of affiliated clans. These affiliated matrilineal descent categories are said to have become affiliated in several different ways:

> The numerical increase of the clans is not due to the process of segmentation of existing clans, but to one of adoption of new

peoples which were met in the course of the journey to the present habitat of the tribe. Accordingly, the phratry is eliminated, in fact, it is unknown to the Navajo, who makes no such distinction. Each clan, therefore, forms a separate whole, which is socially the equal of others with whom it is perchance affiliated by consanguinity or adoption. (Franciscan Fathers 1910: 425.)

While the links connecting various clans into nine or more categories of affiliated clans have their origin in various acts of solidarity, the unity of the matrilineal clan or category itself is based on a chain of mother-child relationships. The specific act utilized for defining matrilineal descent categories is that of giving birth. A child is given the same matrilineal descent identity as its mother by birth. The sole exception occurs when a child is found or is taken captive and its mother is not known. In such an unusual circumstance, the child may be assigned to the clan of its mother by rearing, or to no clan at all; or, if it is a female, she may start a clan of her own.

A matrilineal descent category is described as "da'aholchihigii" (those who are linked together by a chain of births). Because only women give birth, the connecting links are limited to mother-child connections. Thus it is clear that the Navajo descent system abstracts the mother-child relationship from the genealogical network, and categorizes together all those whose mothers have the same descent identity. Navajo descent categories based on the descent relationship between mother and child are thus both unilineal and inclusive.

Matrilineal descent categories are named. A few examples are "many goats," "salt," "red-in-the-water," "edgewater," and "yucca fruit drawn out in a line." The general concept of a matrilineal clan is described as "dine'e" (a particular kind of Navajo). This comes from the base noun "dine" (the people or the Navajo). When a Navajo asks another Navajo about his matrilineal descent identity, he usually says, "Ha'at'iish dine'e nili?" ("What kind of Navajo are you?"). Thus the tribe is dine, and is divided into some sixty or so matrilineal descent categories called dine'e. The nine or more groups of affiliated clans are not named.

The effective and functional meanings attached to common matrilineal descent identity are basically threefold: (1) exogamy, (2) hospitality, and (3) ceremonial cooperation. Specifically, this means two persons who have the same matrilineal descent identity should not marry or experience sexual intercourse, should provide food and lodging for each other while one or the other is traveling away from home, and should help each other during a ceremony for one or the other.[2] These acts of solidarity realize the affective and functional meanings of the concept of matrilineal descent.

The categories of matrilineal descent do not exhaust the total set of categories found in the Navajo descent system. Navajo culture also defines a child as a descendant of its father. The father-child relationship of descent is also utilized in formulating descent categories. All children whose fathers are members of the salt clan are put into a descent category called "those born for the salt clan." "Born for" is the linguistic description of the father-child relationship according to descent reckonings. This category, however, excludes the father, and is therefore not patrilineal. If a father is of the salt clan, his children are born for the salt clan. The category of "those born for the salt clan" includes only one unit, the child, of the dyadic descent relationship between father and child. Therefore, although a child acquires descent identity from its father, the child is not placed in the same descent category as its father.

The Navajo describe this descent category as "ahidadiilchinigii" ("those who are born together"). This term really means "those of many clans who are born together by having fathers of the same matrilineal descent category." The affective and functional meanings which are a part of this descent category are the same as those of the matrilineal descent categories. Those who are born for the same clan are not to marry, but are to be hospitable to each other and to give each other help in ceremonies. Though the same, these bonds of solidarity are weaker than those of the matrilineal categories, because the descent relationship on which this category is based (father-child) is a weaker one than that on which matrilineal categories are based (mother-child).

Descent categories formulated from the father-child relationship are not lineal and are exclusive. The child does not acquire the same identity as its father, and thus the father is excluded from the category. The child does not pass either identity onto his children, and so the category is in no sense lineal. But it is, nevertheless, a descent category—and an important one. It is this kind of descent category which is often overlooked by those who are looking only for unilineal descent groups called clans.

An individual Navajo has two basic descent identities which signify both his maternal and his paternal origin. His relationship to these categories differ from one another. Navajo often say, "Ashįįhi ("mother's clan") ei shima 'adaat 'e" ("Those of my mother's clan are my mothers"). The person, as a cultural construct, of one's mother's matrilineal descent category is one's mother. Accordingly, a Navajo may consider anyone in his mother's category to be a mother, even a man. It is possible but unusual to observe two men address each other as "shima" ("my mother"). Most often, however, when two men of the same clan meet, they each say "those of the salt clan (mother's clan) are my mothers." In this way, they both note to each other that each stands in the position of a mother to the other.

A Navajo may also consider those of his own matrilineal descent category to be his siblings, because all those of his category can consider themselves to be the descendants of a common ancestor. Nevertheless, the mother-child bond is closer and stronger, and a Navajo usually prefers to think of his relationship to others in this category in terms of the mother-child bond rather than of the sibling-sibling bond.

Those who are born for the same clan consider themselves to be siblings because of their common paternal origin. It is interesting to note that those who have the same descent identity, whether matrilineal or paternal origin, consider themselves to be related to each other either as mother and child or as siblings. This indicates that mothers and children or siblings are considered to possess an essential oneness of identity. This essential oneness, as mentioned before, means three kinds of solidary action: (1) exogamy, (2) hospitality, and (3) ceremonial cooperation.

Although each Navajo possesses only two descent identities, he is related to many more descent categories. For example, a Navajo is placed in only one matrilineal descent category, but he is related to a large number of other matrilineal descent categories. A Navajo is related to his father's matrilineal descent category by affinity and paternal descent. A Navajo mother's clan is related to his father's clan by affinity. Because a child's father is an affinal relative of the child's mother and her clansmen and because the child is one of those clansmen, the father is related to his child by affinity.

According to matrilineal descent ideology alone, a child is related to its father's clan by affinity. But, as shown earlier, matrilineal descent does not exhaust the Navajo descent system. There are also descent relationships recognized between fathers and children. Children are considered to be descendants of their father's clan, and the descent identity which results from common paternity is used to define nonlineal, exclusive descent categories. Thus a Navajo often says, "Tł'izi łani (father's clan) ei shizhe'e 'adaat'e" ("Those of my father's clan are my fathers").

A Navajo also considers those born for his own clan to be his children, and those who are born for this clan consider him and all his clansmen to be their fathers. This indicates that the descendants of the women of a particular matrilineal clan are incorporated into the clan, and are related to the clan by the mother-child bond. The children of the men of a matrilineal clan are also considered to be the children of the clan, and are related to the clan by the father-child bond; the children of male clansmen are not incorporated into the clan, but are placed in a separate and distinct category of those born for the clan. Those in the "born for" category are paternal children of the clan, and are related to each other as siblings. So far a Navajo is related to four descent categories, which he considers to be his mothers, fathers, siblings, and children.

A Navajo also considers all those of his maternal grandfather's matrilineal clan to be his maternal grandfathers. Thus Navajo often say "Totsohnii (maternal grandfather's clan) ei shicheii adaat'e" ("Those of my maternal grandfather's clan are my maternal grandfathers"). Likewise, a Navajo considers all those of his paternal grandfather's matrilineal clan to be his paternal grandfathers. Like his relationship to his father's clan, he is related to both his maternal grandfather's and paternal grandfather's clans by affinity and descent.

The maternal grandfather is an affine of ego's clan and, as such, is an affine of ego. In addition, however, ego is considered a descendant of his maternal grandfather's clan, and is thus related to this clan by descent. Ego's relationship to his paternal grandfather's clan involves two links of affinity and two links of descent, making this the descent category to which ego is least strongly related.

The six different descent categories to which ego is related are outlined in figure 2. The four numbers in each of the descent categories indicate various things. A plus beside number one indicates that ego is assigned to, or placed in, that category. A minus indicates that ego is not placed in that category. Thus ego is placed only in descent categories one and two. Number two indicates the basis of ego's relationship to each descent category. Number three indicates the nature or type of the category. Number four indicates the primary way in which ego applies kin terms to each of the descent categories as conceptual units.

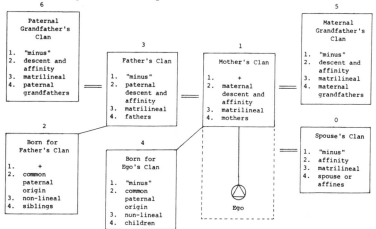

Figure 2. Ego's relationship to seven basic descent categories. (Note: There are more Navajo descent categories; the ones given here are the more important ones.)

It should also be noted here that all affiliated clans are conceived of as a unit. Thus, not only everyone in ego's mother's matrilineal category but all those of clans affiliated with ego's clan may be considered mothers. Those born for different but affiliated clans also consider themselves to be siblings. Thus ego is not related to only seven categories, but to at least forty or fifty, because each of the seven categories to which ego is related by descent or affinity has affiliated categories.

Another important point, and one on which there has been much confusion, is how the Navajo descent system governs marriage. The traditional approach is summarized by Kluckhohn and Leighton:

> Each Navajo belongs to the clan of his mother, but it must not
> be forgotten that he is equally spoken of as "born for" the
> clan of his father. The father's clansmen are all considered to be
> relatives. . . . One may never marry within one's own clan or one's
> father's. (1962: 112.)

Others (Shepardson 1963: 35; Aberle 1961: 109; Hill 1943: 16), in line with this tradition, report that marriages into the father's clan are prohibited.

Gladys Reichard reported that marriages into the father's clan were preferred (1928: 65). Informants of Carr, Spencer, and Woolley at Pueblo Alto failed to mention any prohibition against marriage into the father's clan (1939: 255). My own informants at Rough Rock differed on the issue.[3] Some said that marriages into the father's clan were all right, but that most objected to such marriages. Everyone has found extensive joking about sexual relations with cross-cousins. Navajo boys use the term "shizeedi" ("cross-cousin of the opposite sex") as a term for lover or sweetheart. One of the Enemyway songs implies sexual relations between cross-cousins.

Aberle (1961: 192–96) and Zelditch (1959: 470–89) have tried to solve this problem with statistics. They have gone through most of the available data and calculated the percentage of actual marriages into the father's clan. Because statistically such marriages are few, Aberle concludes that such "marriages are so infrequent as to support the view of those ethnologists who state that the relationship is prohibited (1961: 194)."

As a means of solving this problem, neither the "view of those ethnologists" nor the statistics are of much help. To understand how a Navajo is related to his father's clan, we must look for the answer in the concepts and relationships of Navajo kinship as a cultural system. The cultural concepts discussed in chapter 4 make it clear that a Navajo is related to his father's clan by both affinity and descent. This dual relationship provides the Navajo with a number of alternatives. He may ignore the relationship of descent and see his father's clanswomen as ideal affinal relatives, or he may wish to emphasize the relationship of descent with his father's clan. Most informants emphasize the descent aspect of the relationship, but some, particularly those who have married into the father's clan or have sweethearts there, emphasize the affinal aspect of the relationship.

The maternal grandfather in the Navajo system is also related to his grandchildren by both affinity and descent. The maternal grandfather is recognized as a relative by descent. He is called "hacheii" and is referred to as "hak'ei" ("relative by descent"). The maternal grandfather is also an affinal relative of ego's matrilineal clan, and ego, and his fellow clansmen sometimes refer to him as "ayehe" ("inmarrying affine").

Even though ego considers all the members of his maternal grandfather's clan as hacheii and hak'ei, ego often emphasizes his affinal bond to this clan. No ethnographer has reported a prohibition against marriage into this clan. That is because Navajo tend to emphasize (with regard to marriage considerations) the affinal bond over the descent bond with the maternal grandfather's clansmen. In the father's clan, the descent bond tends to be emphasized because it is given special recognition by the "born for" concept.

There is an interesting event in the autobiography *Son of Old Man Hat* which illustrates the dual relationship to the maternal grandfather's clan and the different ways in which this dual relationship can be manipulated by the Navajo:

> Then another girl grabbed me. . . . I asked about her clan and her father's clan. She said, "My father's clan is Bitter Water, and my clan is Salt." While she was holding me a fellow said, "She's your granddaughter, because her mother's father belongs to your clan." So she let me go. . . .
>
> I was about to go to sleep when the same girl grabbed me. I said "You're my granddaughter." But she kept pulling on me, and so I danced with her. I tried to get away, but she held me tight as she could and started dragging and pulling me out of the dance to where her mother and others were sitting. Her mother shook hands with me, and I said, "What's the matter with this girl? She's my granddaughter. . . ." Her mother laughed and said, "Well, she must like you, and if she does, go with her, because she's always wanted to marry a man of my father's clan. So you can take her right now."
>
> I tried to take the girl's hand away, but she was hanging onto me as tight as she could. Her mother said, "Well, my father, we'll go home tonight." (Dyk 1938: 360.)

Aberle's discussion of joking relationships also verifies the affinal relationship to one's father's, maternal grandfather's, or paternal grandfather's clans. Aberle states that when a joke is aimed at ego's sister's spouse, then ego will take some article of clothing from the one making the joke. The sister's husband is of course an affine, and the exchange is part of the affinal bond. Aberle also indicates that the same thing is true when someone makes a joke about ego's father's clan or clansmen. Ego will take a piece of clothing from the one who makes the joke. In both cases, the joke is made about an affinal relative, either a sister's spouse or a father's clansman. (1961: 155.)

In summary, we can say that the Navajo descent system is

bilateral, formulating unilineal, inclusive categories on the mother's side and nonlineal, exclusive categories on the father's side. A Navajo is also related to four additional categories by a combination of affinity and descent, two of which utilize the father-child relationship, while the other two utilize the maternal grandfather-grandchild and the paternal grandfather-grandchild relationships. A Navajo is also related by affinity to his spouse's clan and to the clans of all the spouses of his clansmen. With all these possible relationships, it is not surprising that any two Navajo may be related to each other in several different ways by the concepts and categories of the Navajo descent system (Dyk 1938: 364).

Another important aspect of the Navajo descent system is that none of the descent categories is utilized in the formation of a social group which meets together, takes collective action, or holds property. Instead, the cultural categories of the descent system are given other meanings in the social system, and these meanings can be summarized as threefold: (1) exogamy, (2) hospitality, and (3) ceremonial cooperation.

In this chapter, there has been an attempt to study the Navajo descent system culturally. The cultural study of descent focuses on the way in which descent categories are formulated, defined, and differentiated, and how those within a descent category are related to each other and to those units and categories outside their category. Descent categories may be utilized in different ways and given different meanings in various social systems, only one of which involves the formation of descent groups.

Even though all those of ego's mother's descent category are considered mothers, all those of ego's father's descent category are considered fathers, and so on, kinsmen are futher distinguished and differentiated by the concepts or features of sex, generation, relative age, and lineal or collateral distance. Although the giving of life and the sharing of sustenance found in the mother-child bond provide the basic behavioral code for all kinship relations, this code is modified when the attributes of sex, generation, sibling order or relative age, and distance are taken into consideration. The nature of these modifications is discussed in the following chapter.

# 6    The Concepts of Sex, Generation, Sibling Order, and Distance

In Navajo kinship, relatives of the same sex enjoy greater solidarity than similar relatives of the opposite sex. There are two major reasons for this. One is related to Durkheim's notion of mechanical solidarity. The division of labor according to sex in Navajo culture more closely relates relatives of the same sex, and tends to differentiate relatives of opposite sexes. During the discussion before the separation of the sexes in underworld mythology, the sexual division of labor is mentioned:

> "It is we who clear the fields and help to till them, we kill game for you, and guide and assist you in your labors. . . ." To this the women answer, "We till the soil and carry the water; we make the fire and weave the blankets; we can take care of ourselves. . . ." (MA 209). In another version of this quarrel the chief's wife holds that "the women did more work than the men, for they tilled the fields, made the clothing, cared for the children, and did the cooking, while the men did practically nothing. . . ." (CA 85). Or the chief's wife declares, "It is we women who till the fields and gather food; we can live on the produce of our fields, and the seeds and fruits we collect" (MD 218, n. 32) (Spencer 1947: 24.)

This discussion led to the separation of the sexes. When the women found that they could not live without the men, the sexes regrouped and the men were designated as the leaders (Spencer 1947: 36). In fact, nearly all the chiefs and leaders of the people in mythology were men. The major roles of women were defined in terms of reproducing and sustaining life. Men were the leaders in political and religious affairs. This leadership role of men, as opposed to the reproductive role of women, is brought out in the following mythological fragment collected by Werner and Begishe:

> 4. dibe dahazlii' jo aadoo dibe binahat'a silii jini. dajiniigo haala yit'eego haajila alaah nitsekees dooleeł, ba diih doolghee, hodooniis, jini.

[4. After sheep have come into existence, they say. It was said, "Who will be in what way the foremost thinker, man or woman?" "Prepare a smoke for them," it was said, they say.]

5. aadoo shii inda yooɬgaii nat'ostse', dootɬ'izhii nat'osts'ęeni' ei dįihgo diihyilya, dineji yeedeeyol nilei haadishįi yak'aash bąahdi dįi'di aɬk'ihneet'i' silįi' jiri.
[5. The smoke was prepared in a white shell pipe and a turquoise pipe. As for the man, he started to blow and the smoke extended four times around the horizon, they say.]

6. aadoo inda t'aa ako naana ashdzanishą'hodooniid nit'ęe' t'aa aghiidigii ahee' nijool doo t'aa ako nilei bitɬ'ehgone' i'iijoo jini.]
[6. And then it was said that woman was next. The smoke went just a little way, turned around and disappeared there between her crotch, they say.]

7. 'eiiga' t'ei' yaanitsekees dooleeɬ la hodooniid jini.
[7. "That is really what she would think of most," it was said, they say.] (Werner and Begishe 1968: 57–58.)

Another major distinction in the roles of males and females is found in the reproductive process. Here, as underworld mythology teaches, male and female roles are distinct but complementary, and one is worthless without the other. Thus a major function of sexual differences is found in their complementary roles in sexual intercourse and reproduction.

A necessary by-product of the fact that sexual differences are fundamentally important to the primary symbol of affinal solidarity is the lack of solidarity across sex lines outside or beyond primary affinal solidarity (marriage). In simple terms, the fact that one being is a male and another a female permits them to marry and experience sexual intercourse—the primary affinal bond. However, outside this primary bond, a husband and a wife have affinal relatives with whom they are prohibited by rules of adultery to realize their affinal bond in sexual intercourse. By not being permitted to express their affinal solidarity in a natural but improper way, tension often occurs between affines of the opposite sex, which is handled by limiting their contact with one another.

In the most extreme case of affinal closeness, son-in-law and mother-in-law, this tension results in sexual avoidance by the son-in-law not looking upon the mother-in-law (Aberle 1961: 150–51). Further, if a man's sister-in-law is married, he must be careful not to allow himself to be found alone with her, or her husband will suspect him of adultery. If his sister-in-law is not married, he must be careful not to be found alone with her, because his wife will get jealous.

This weakening of the solidarity between opposite sexes because of sexual avoidance is even more true among those related by kinship. Brothers and sisters must avoid touching each other, passing items directly to each other, and being found alone together. In addition, brothers and sisters must not even use the duoplural forms of verbs in referring to things they did together. Brothers and sisters, mothers and sons, and fathers and daughters must not joke with each other about sexual matters. Thus the differences in sex which are so necessary for primary affinal solidarity weaken secondary affinal solidarity and all kinship solidarity.

From these cultural concepts, it can be said that mothers and daughters are slightly more solidary than mothers and sons, that fathers and sons are slightly more solidary than fathers and daughters, and that brothers and brothers or sisters and sisters are slightly more solidary than brothers and sisters, and so on.

This weakening of opposite sex solidarity diminishes in proportion to the number of generations existing between two relatives of the opposite sex. For instance, although a son may not joke about sexual matters with a sister or a mother, he may do so casually with a grandmother. This relationship is evident in mythology:

> The hero of Prostitution way teases his grandmother about her resplendent visitor, Talking God (Prostitution H). In Navajo culture this relationship permits joking of a sexual nature, and it may be significant that the two stories in which the hero undertakes sexual exploits on his own initiative are those in which he lives only with a grandmother (Water, Prostitution) (Spencer 1957: 68–69.)

The fact that the only kinship terms on the mother's side which do not distinguish sex are those which grandparents use for grandchildren may also indicate the lesser degree of importance of sexual differences among kinsmen separated by at least two generations. It should also be pointed out that the relations between father and daughter and mother and son are not as weakened by sexual differences as those between brother and sister or between cross-cousins.[1] This, however, is not the only, or even the most important, aspect of generational differences in Navajo kinship.

Another structural principle with regard to the concepts of generation in Navajo culture is what Radcliffe-Brown, in a discussion of African kinship systems, has called "the merging of alternate generations" (Radcliffe-Brown and Forde 1950: 29). Radcliffe-Brown notes that the normal relationship between parents and children is that of superordination and subordination. The subordinate position of children requires them to respect their parents, and usually requires parents to support, care for, discipline, and instruct their children. This subordinate-superordinate relationship, however, does not hold true for grandparents and grandchildren:

> If the exercise of authority on the one side and respect and obedience on the other were simply, or even primarily, a matter of relative age, we should expect to find these features markedly characteristic of the relations between grandparents and grandchildren. Actually we find most commonly something almost the opposite of this, a relation of friendly familiarity and almost of social equality. . . . One aspect of the structural principle with which we are here concerned is that one generation is replaced in course of time by the generation of their grandchildren. . . . This may sometimes result in what may be called the merging of alternate generations. (1950: 29.)

These features of generational differences are prominent in Navajo culture too. The term for maternal grandfather is also used as the term for friend. Self-reciprocal terms exist between paternal grandparents and their grandchildren. The familiarity of the maternal grandmother to her grandchildren has already been noted in the fact that some joking of a sexual content may occur between her grandson and herself. In my experience, grandparents seldom discipline; when they do, it is in a casual manner with regard to minor cases of misbehavior.

There are, however, some circumstances in which grandparents discipline their grandchildren. These circumstances occur when grandparents are acting as parents—that is, when they are rearing their grandchildren. It is important to note that when grandparents rear their grandchildren, they call each other by parent-child terms.

The relationship between relatives separated by more than two generations is similar but slightly weaker than the relationship between relatives separated by two generations.

Relatives of the same generation are differentiated by the concepts of age or sibling order. Younger siblings are subordinate to older siblings, and in many situations it seems that the eldest brother is a second father in the household and that an older sister is a second mother. My experience in living for extended periods of time in five different Navajo households strongly illustrated to me the importance of sibling order. The oldest sibling (alaaji naaghahigii) and the youngest sibling (naak'eeschąą'i) are of particular interest, because the oldest has no one above him and the youngest has no one below him. Another factor which suggests the importance of sibling order is that many Navajo can recall the exact sibling order of a set of siblings who have been dead for as long as a hundred years. As far back as their memories take them in their genealogies, they can remember the order in which siblings were born.

It should also be noted that sibling order is entirely defined by, and traced according to, relationships to a single mother. Although all kinds of siblings differentiate themselves terminologically according to age, the concept of sibling order ('ałkee hajee) refers to the order in which siblings come out of the same womb. Another word used for sibling order is "ałkee naakai," which refers to the order in which they walk and has nothing necessarily to do with birth.

If a child is reared by a mother who gave birth to several other children, the child by rearing only will be placed in the sibling order with no stigma attached. One can even ask a fellow sibling if such a sibling came up out of the same womb as he did, and the sibling will most often say yes, even though further interrogation will eventually get him to say no. On the other hand, children born to the same mother but not raised by her are often left out of the sibling group unless the informant is really pushed to include all those born together even though they were not reared together. Siblings of different fathers are not distinguished in any way in the sibling order, and siblings of the same father but different mothers constitute no sibling order at all. The sibling order can thus be defined as the way in which the children by birth or by rearing of a single mother are differentiated according to age and/or order of birth.

The concept of distance is also important in defining and differentiating Navajo categories of kinship and affinity. Some anthropologists have attempted to articulate a concept of distance which is accurate and appropriate for all kinship systems. The concept of distance articulated by Radcliffe-Brown is a popular one:

> Relationships of the first order are those within the elementary family, viz. the relation of parent and child, that of husband and wife, and that between siblings. Relationships of the second order are those traced through one connecting person such as those with father's father, mother's brother, stepmother (father's wife), sister's husband, brother's son, wife's father, etc. Those of the third order have two connecting links, as mother's brother's son, father's sister's husband, and so on. (Radcliffe-Brown and Forde 1950: 6.)

Although these concepts of distance may be appropriate for some kinship systems, they are certainly not appropriate for the Navajo. The general principle that distance is marked off by the number of linking categories is true for the Navajo, but the way in which categories are linked in the Navajo system greatly differs from the concepts of distance which some anthropologists have imposed upon the Navajo system. The number of linking categories between various categories of kinship and affinity are shown in figure 3.

Only the relationship of husband-wife and mother-child are primary, and involve no connecting category. The relationships of father-child, sibling-sibling, and maternal grandmother-maternal grandchild are all connected by one category, the mother. These are secondary relationships. Ego and his paternal grandmother and maternal grandmother's husband, children, or mother (ego's maternal great-grandmother) are all relationships of the third order, and so on.

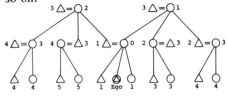

Key:  0 = primary relationship
      1 = one linking category
      2 = two linking categories
      3 = three linking categories
      4 = four linking categories
      5 = five linking categories

Figure 3. The number of linking categories between ego and various kinsmen

It is interesting to note the distance between ego and his cousins. His matrilateral parallel cousins have three connecting categories.

Matrilateral and patrilateral cross-cousins are linked to ego by four connecting categories. Ego's patrilateral parallel cousins are linked to ego through five connecting categories. By the popular scheme of distance, all these cousin categories would have been considered to be the same distance from ego. But concepts of distance, like those of sex, generation, and sibling order, must be defined within the culture and not imposed or assumed.

# 7 Kinship and Affinal Solidarity as Symbolized in the Enemyway

Kinship solidarity was defined in chapter 2 by the general concepts of giving and sharing. Nonkinship solidarity was defined in chapter 3 by the general concepts of exchange or reciprocity. Both solidarity based on giving or sharing and solidarity based on exchange or reciprocity involve the acting unit in both giving and receiving. Nevertheless, there are fundamental differences in these two kinds of solidary behavior. Giving is unilateral, while exchange is reciprocal. Parents give to their children with little thought of return. Although children sometimes help their parents in old age, children give most to their own children and they receive most from their parents. Thus kinsmen often give to one set of kinsmen and receive from another, but there is no set system to make it an equilibrium. The factor of need, not the factors of balance or equal exchange, is of primary concern. Kinsman A gives to Kinsman B because he is in need and not because he expects something equal in return. If Kinsman B does give something in return, it will not be because Kinsman A gave B something earlier; it will be because A is in need of help.

An infant is to a great extent helpless. By Navajo concepts, she who helps it is its mother. It was shown earlier that the mother-child bond is the primary bond of Navajo kinship, and that all kinsmen are merely differentiated kinds of mothers. The life and sustenance mothers provide for their children are the primary symbols of kinship solidarity, and it is from this relationship that the nature of kinship solidarity in Navajo culture becomes clear. Navajo mothers do not give life, food, and loving care to their children because they want the same in return. A mother loves and helps her child regardless of whether he is a king or a bum, a worker or an indolent, a helper or one who is helpless, a contributor or a parasite, moral or immoral. A mother continues to love when she is hated, and continues to give when her gifts are not appreciated. Hers is the highest form of human solidarity, and it is on this relationship that Navajo kinship is based.

Nonkinship solidarity involves systems of exchange or reciprocity, and is of a very different nature. Here equity of exchange is paramount, and need is ignored. This form of reciprocity is voluntary and contractual, based on mutual agreements and obligations. A will give to B if B will agree to return something of equal value to A. A gives only because he expects something in return. Systems of exchange may also be circular; A gives to B, who gives to C, who gives to D, who gives back to A.

The primary bond of nonkinship solidarity in Navajo culture is found in the husband-wife relationship. When a husband is a bum, or an indolent, or immoral, the wife usually gets rid of him. If a wife is barren, a husband goes elsewhere. If either sees the relationship as without merit to himself or herself, it will likely be dissolved. The relationship is supposed to be 'advantageous to both through mutual obligations of assistance. Where one party falters, the relationship loses its balance and disintegrates.

Whereas nonkinship solidarity is weak, specific, and terminable, kinship solidarity in Navajo culture is intense, diffuse, and enduring. The kinship group is bound together by the latter form of solidarity, and the dine (the people or the Navajo) are bound together by the former kind of solidarity which exists across the boundaries of kinship. These concepts and forms of solidarity are all dramatized in the Enemyway,[1] at which a relatively brief look would be worthwhile at this point.

In comparison with other Navajo ceremonials, Enemyway may not be considered by casual observers to be much more than a minor ritual. It features no sand paintings, no prayer sticks, and no masked dancers. White people call it the "squaw dance," and consider it some type of party or recreational activity. To many whites, it probably seems something like a New Year's Eve party. Nevertheless, behind the gaiety, the group singing, the dancing, and the socializing, ritual activities of major importance are occurring.

The personnel, time, and cost required for the performance of the Enemyway are external indications of the meaning of the ceremony to most Navajo. In the ritual activities alone, more than thirty different persons are required. When to this is added the many others who are required for the more laborious tasks of construction, hauling of firewood, preparation of food, and so on, there are far more than a hundred persons required to carry out the ritual. By adding the spectators to this number, there becomes an average of more than five hundred involved in the ritual performance.

From initial planning to completion, the ritual requires around two weeks, with the last three days containing the major aspects of the ritual. By assuming that the ritual is performed an average of five times each summer in each community, and with approximately one hundred Navajo communities, it is likely that the ritual occurs five hundred times each summer. An average of two thousand dollars is spent or exchanged in the performance of each ritual, and so it is likely that a million dollars is spent yearly by Navajo in the performance of the Enemyway.

As with nearly all Navajo ceremonies, the Enemyway is designed to cure patients, who are are ill because they are bothered by ghosts or spirits of dead ana'i (non-Navajo), often considered the result of too much contact with non-Navajo. The Enemyway is an attack on the ghost of the alien which is causing the illness, and the victorious attack, dramatized in the ritual, cures the patients.

There are two main symbols in the Enemyway rite. One is the rattlestick; the other is the scalp. The rattlestick is a symbol of the dine, and the scalp is a symbol of the ana'i. The term "dine" marks the boundary of and is a linguistic symbol of Navajo society, which comprises a group of Navajo who are bound together by combinations of kinship and nonkinship solidarity.

One of the major forms of nonkinship solidarity upon which Navajo society is built is that of mutual assistance in warfare. Dine are not to fight against each other, and are to help each other when attacked by an outsider. As in Sandoval's group at Canoncito, Navajo who broke from the main body and participated in attacks  on the dine were called ana'i. In at least one sense, the reciprocal alliance called dine is like a marriage. When one group fails to fulfill its obligations by attacking instead of assisting the others, then a divorce occurs and the bond of mutual assistance in warfare is destroyed.

The nonkinship solidarity of the dine is further enhanced by a system of exchange. The rules of exogamy compel the exchange of men and/or women among kin groups. Other exchanges involve goods, services, and food. The importance of exchange as a symbol of the nonkinship solidarity of the dine forms a major part of the Enemyway ceremonial.

In the performance of the Enemyway, a dual organization suddenly arises. One group is formed around the chief patient, and is made up of his kinsmen. The other group is formed around the stick receiver, and consists of those who are related to him by kinship. In most cases, a Navajo can find a kinship tie to either leader, and joins the group to which he feels closest or the one to which he has been requested to give assistance.

The patient's kin group assembles several days before the ceremony begins and chooses a nonkinsman of the patient to be the stick receiver. Most often the stick receiver is someone from another chapter (community). The primary idea in making the choice is to select a person and a group with whom the patient and his group have little contact or relations but with whom they would like to establish some stronger bonds of reciprocal solidarity. When a person is chosen to be the stick receiver, a delegation from the patient's group goes to the selected person's home and requests that he be the stick receiver. If he accepts, as is most often the case, the delegation returns home and announces the acceptance of the person chosen to be the stick receiver. Preparations are then finalized for the performance of the ceremony.

On the first day of the ceremony, the rattlestick is prepared at the home of the chief patient. During the late afternoon, the chief patient and his kin group begin the journey to the home of the stick receiver. They normally arrive there just before sunset and present the rattlestick to its selected receiver. He inspects it to see if it is properly prepared. If it is, he accepts it and sings some Blessingway songs. The stick, the cars, and the horses of the patient's group have yarn attached to them, which is later distributed among the stick receiver's group.

After these initial presentations, the patient's group camps together about a hundred yards from the stick receiver's group. The stick receiver's group then provides food for the visiting group. Shortly after sundown, the all-night singing and dancing begin. All dances are girls' choices, and the boys must pay the girls for the dances. Those of the same clan or other close kinship relations may not dance with each other.

On the morning of the second day, the patient's group is presented with gifts by the stick receiver's group. After these gifts are received, the patient's group returns home. On the evening of the second day, the stick receiver's group moves to within a few miles of the patient's home. There they camp all night. All-night singing and dancing again occur.

About sunrise on the final day, the stick receiver's group makes a mock attack on the patient's home. Afterward, the stick receiver's group camps at a separate place designated for them. They are brought food from the patient's group. After eating they assemble in front of the ceremonial hogan, and the patient's group distributes gifts among them. The next major event is the "blackening" ceremony, which is culminated by the attack on the scalp. Following this, the people eat again, perform the circle dance, and have a final night of singing and dancing.

The structure of the Enemyway is highly revealing. First, the dine are opposed to the ana'i. Second, the dine consist of two groups which form a dual organization in the performance of the ritual. Solidarity within each of the groups is based on kinship ties; solidarity across the two groups takes the reciprocal form of nonkinship solidarity. The relations between the dine and the ana'i are considered the antithesis of solidarity. Power over the enemy ghost is achieved through tribal unity, which is based on both kinship and nonkinship solidarity.

The internal unity and solidarity of the kin group are demonstrated in the Enemyway ritual in a number of ways. The cost in time, materials, food, and money is shared by the patient's kin group. No kinsman is paid or reimbursed for any service rendered. The women of the patient's kin group provide the yarn for the rattlestick. The patient's kinsmen are separated in the shelter shade from his wife's kinsmen. The male patient associates only with his own kinsmen and not with his wife's kinsmen. Temporarily, the marriage bond is overriden, and the husband and wife ideally do not associate with each other and should not sit beside each other or be near each other. In other words, the patient's bond or solidarity with his own kin group is emphasized over his marital bond.

The stick receiver's kin group also has its separate camp. Eating together is a symbol of solidarity. The important aspect of the separate accommodations for each kin group is that this amounts to each eating in its own place, demonstrating its solidarity. Food is shared freely within each of the kin groups. All this indicates that solidarity within the kin groups is realized in acts of sharing.

The solidarity across the lines of kinship or between the two groups is framed in terms of reciprocity. These reciprocal relations involve a set of exchanges. The rattlestick, the yarn, and the drum are ceremonial items involved in these exchanges. The gift exchange is probably the single most important expression and realization of the nonkinship solidarity between the two groups. The exchange of food is also important, and must not be overlooked.

Every relationship across the boundaries of kinship is framed according to the concept of reciprocity. Girls must dance with boys who are not of their clan, and these boys must pay them for the dance. Where romance leads to sexual relations, exchange must occur. Patients are "blackened" by nonkinsmen, and they must exchange gifts.

The two kin groups are united under the concept of dine, which are opposed to the ana'i. The dine are symbolized by the rattlestick; the ana'i, by the scalp. These two dominant symbols provide a condensation of almost the entire content and meaning of the myth and ritual. They also provide a polarization of meaning (Turner 1967: 28). Let us examine each of these dominant symbols in detail.

The rattlestick is obtained and decorated on the first day of the rite. A reliable and knowledgeable person is sent out to cut a cedar stick approximately three feet long. After singing a song and saying a prayer, he cuts the stick in a sunwise fashion, beginning at the east side. The stick is returned to the ceremonial hogan, where it is placed vertically in a ceremonial basket. The stick decorator then begins his work.

The first design put on the stick is that of the extended bowstring. It symbolizes Monster Slayer and the power he had over his enemies the monsters. Its source is the Sun, the father of the Twins and all Navajo. The second design put on the stick is that of the outline of Changing Woman's hair bun at the time she gave birth to the Twins. This design symbolizes Born for the Water. Its source is Changing Woman or Earth Woman, the mother of the Twins and all Navajo. One is thus a symbol of power, and the other is a symbol of life, especially its sustenance and reproduction. These two designs are shown in figure 4.

Born for the Water          Monster Slayer

Figure 4. Symbols on Enemyway prayerstick

Next, the stick decorator rubs the entire stick with tallow that has been mixed with charred herbs and kneaded into a ball. The burning of the herbs of the earth symbolizes the killing of the monsters by Monster Slayer. In the myth, Monster Slayer covered his body with this black tallow after killing all the monsters. The charred herbs are also symbolic of the old vegetation covering the earth's surface.

The stick is next rubbed with tallow which has been mixed with red ocher, symbolic of the blood of the monsters which con-taminated the earth and its vegetation. At the same time, this redness is also a symbol of the menstrual blood of Changing Woman and the reproductive capacities of all females. It is thus a "uni-fication of disparate significata" (Turner 1967: 28). It symbolizes the contamination of the old life and vegetation of the earth, while also symbolizing the capacity of the earth and living beings to reproduce a newness of life and vegetation.

The stick is next wrapped with fresh, unburned vegetation (grama grass, red grass, sage, dodgeweed, spruce, and gray willow). This vegetation symbolizes the new, purified vegetation of the earth, and is wrapped with strips of buckskin from an unwounded deer. Gladys Reichard, in her *Navajo Religion: A Study of Symbolism*, makes this statement concerning buckskin:

> Buckskin taken from a deer killed with pollen—that is, without wounding—is an important ceremonial article. . . .
> Mythologically buckskin is an emblem of life; ritualistically it is a life symbol. Creation, really transformation, was accomplished by laying corn, precious stones, or both between buckskins. Restoration is brought about in much the same way—the properties and procedure are almost identical for transformation from inanimate to animate and for restoration from unconsciousness or death to life.
> Bits of Rainboy's body were assembled on one buckskin and another was laid over the parts. A rite with buckskin, described in the Bead Chant myth, transformed feathers into animals whose skins have since been a chant property. Two buckskins figured in the preparation of seed for planting, the rite signifying life and transformation. (1950: 530.)

In the midst of the various herbs, yellow turkey feathers are placed. The turkey is considered an ally of the dine, to whom she gave seed for domestic plants. In the myth of the Night Chant, the turkey dropped seeds of corn, pumpkin, watermelon, muskmelon, and beans from its wings, and taught the boy hero methods of agriculture. The fact that only yellow feathers are used is also significant. Reichard says that yellow corn represents "the power of reproduction and growth. Woman originated from a yellow corn ear; yellow corn meal is a female symbol of domesticated plants. The inexhaustible food bowl is yellow, symbolizing sustenance." (1950: 193.)

Attached to the buckskin strips are eagle tail feathers and deer hooves. These represent strength, speed, and deliverance. Various transformations and creations of beings are accomplished by placing feathers between buckskins. Reichard states that eagles are able to change small game (such as rabbits and prairie dogs) into rare game (such as deer and antelope), and that deer are symbolic of hunting power and methods (1950: 265, 549).

Peppermint and pennyroyal are put in a buckskin pouch and attached to the stick. The odor of these plants is said to attract good and to disperse evil. The description of the scene in which the hero of the Feather Chant first saw deer and other rare game includes the following:

> The land was filled with deer and covered with beautiful flowers. The air had the odor of pollen and fragrant blossoms. Birds of the most beautiful plumage were flying in the air or perching on the flowers and building nests in the deer's antlers. (Reichard 1950: 263.)

Finally, the stick is made ready for use and travel by the looping of a strip of cloth and bands of yarn around it in a sunwise fashion. The yarn, provided by the women of the patient's group, can be of different colors, but the wide strip of cloth must be red. The red cloth is symbolic of the reproductive capacities of women and the blood of the slain enemy. The long strands of yarn are symbols of long life and a lengthy period of reproductive capacity in women. Father Barard Haile's informant says that the yarn also represents the rejoicing of women at the time when reproduction and vegetation were restored to the earth (1938: 74).

We can now see that the rattlestick and its symbolism is a condensation of nearly the entire content, sequence, and meaning of the myth[2] and ritual. The sequence of the myth is matched by the sequence followed in the decoration of the rattlestick. These oppositions are:

| *Rattlestick* | *Scalp* |
|---|---|
| Dine, Navajo | Ana'i, enemy, foreigner |
| Life | Death |
| Good | Evil |
| Power | Weakness |
| Moisture | Dryness |
| New, pure vegetation | Old, impure vegetation |
| Reproduction of life | End of life |
| Capacity for rapid movement | No movement |
| Purity | Contamination, impurity |
| Beauty | Ugliness |

The concept of dine is symbolically realized and opposed to the symbol of the ana'i. During the blackening ceremony, the patient is dressed in the clothes of Monster Slayer and arrayed with the symbols of the life and power of the dine. When this is complete, he goes out and attacks the scalp with a crow bill. Others shoot at it, bury it with ashes, and burn it into nonexistence. This experience provides an enormous release of hostility and a tremendous bolstering of tribal pride and solidarity. Symbolically, the power of the dine over its enemies is asserted and demonstrated. This power comes, in part, from strong tribal solidarity, both kinship and nonkinship.

To summarize, the dine are bound together by kinship and nonkinship forms of solidarity. Kinsmen are differentiated kinds of mothers who give and share according to need. Nonkinsmen are differentiated kinds of affines who exchange for mutual advantage. Kinship is by far the most intense, the most diffuse, and the most enduring form of solidarity among the dine. There is an effort by the Navajo to think of, and to relate to, everyone in terms of kinship. Everyone is addressed as a kinsman; affinal terms and personal names are seldom used.

The cultural ideal of kinship solidarity and the great value placed on it are demonstrated by the fact that some of the worst things that a Navajo can say about another Navajo are: "He acts as though he has no kinsmen" and "She refuses to help her mother or to care for her children." True kinsmen love, share, and give in all circumstances, without any thought of return. To put it simply and concisely, true kinsmen are good mothers, and the love between mother and child is intense, diffuse, and enduring. And that, it seems to me, is what Navajo kinship as a cultural system is all about.

**2**      **Navajo Kinship
as a Social System**

# Introduction
# to Part 2

At the beginning of chapter 1, the cultural system was distinguished from the social system. The entire part I of this book was concerned with the analysis of Navajo kinship as a cultural system. Part II will be devoted to an analysis of Navajo kinship as a social system, involving a switch from concepts, symbols, and meanings to real beings, actions, and networks of actions.

The cultural system is an ideal one, with a logical and coherent structure. Culture provides human beings with a pattern to follow in social relations, and much of human behavior is an enactment of cultural patterns. Nevertheless, human beings live in a real and often disorderly world, and changing environmental factors may compel them to vary their behavior from the ideal. Ecological factors are often important in understanding the organization and operation of a social system.

When environmental factors force substantial changes in the social system, these changes are reconciled with the cultural system. This reconciliation often requires adjustments and changes in the cultural system, but not always. In most cases, deviances from the cultural ideal in the social system are reconciled by a return to the ideal. Culture is therefore a major influence for continuity and stability in social life. Without the stabilizing influence of culture, social systems would be in a constant state of disorder, conflict, and chaos.

Aberle argues that the factors of rapid change, resource instability, expanding population and territory, and the conflicts between acculturation and kinship organization in a tribal society are responsible for the "flexibility" which he and others have found in the Navajo social organization (1963: 7). Although I agree that these environmental factors have tended to produce disorder in Navajo social life, I will try to show that the cultural concepts outlined in part I have produced a high degree of order and stability in Navajo social life, and that much of the so-called flexibility in Navajo social organization is due to an inadequate understanding of Navajo culture and its relationship to Navajo social organization.

# 8     Social Organization in the Rough Rock–Black Mountain Area

Navajoland is the Holy Land of the Navajo people. It is circumscribed by sacred mountains, and is described as being beautiful. Essential parts, as well as the land itself, are called mother. For a Navajo, there is no safer, more secure, and more wonderful place to be than close to Earth Mother within the boundaries of the sacred mountains, which represent parts of her body. Earth Mother, like all good mothers, cares for, protects, and provides for her children. Reichard says there is "a feeling that wherever the mother is, is home" (1928: 51). Navajoland is thus the sacred motherland and homeland of the Navajo.

Some non-Navajo have seen Navajoland as a bleak, lonely, and forbidding place. On the contrary, Navajoland is thought by its people to be as sacred and secure as motherhood itself. Only when he travels outside the boundaries of the sacred mountains does a Navajo feel he is in potentially dangerous land. On many occasions I have noticed a real and definite change in the attitudes, speech, and temperament of Navajo when they reenter Navajoland from travels and activities in the outside world. Places beyond the boundaries of Navajoland are referred to as "tł'oodi" ("outside"). The general oppositions of inside/outside, secure/insecure, and mother/stranger are very much a part of the way Navajo perceive their land as contrasted to those places beyond its boundaries.

The specific place and area where a Navajo and his close relatives live, graze their sheep, and plant their fields are doubly home, doubly secure, and greatly cherished. The specific people with whom I have had the privilege of being acquainted and of whom a brief account will be provided in this section live on or near Black Mountain. They all live in the school district of the Rough Rock Demonstration School. I initially got to know them while working at their school for two years, mainly in the area of community-school relations. After leaving Rough Rock for a year to do graduate study,

I returned in the summer of 1969 to renew my friendship with the poeple of Rough Rock and to continue the research which I had started earlier.

There is no clear, distinct community at Rough Rock. Navajo do not live in villages, and have not organized themselves into local communities until rather recently. Although there were some local leaders or headmen, the area or domain of their leadership was not clearly defined or carefully bounded. In this century, Navajo communities, as local groups of people with common interests, have arisen around trading posts, schools, churches, and chapters. In most cases, the chapter is the strongest force for local community integration. The chapter is the local unit of tribal government, and it is usually the only community institution controlled by the people themselves.

The tribal government began in 1923. It was organized by the Bureau of Indian Affairs in order to produce a "legitimate" body of Navajo who could lease Navajo lands to oil companies for drilling. In the days of stock reduction (1935–45), the reservation was divided into eighteen grazing districts, and later these districts were further divided into slightly more than a hundred chapters. Actually, the local chapters began developing earlier around the institutions previously mentioned, and were later officially recognized by the tribal government.

Many local boundaries are artificial, and conflict with one another. This is particularly true at Rough Rock. The beginning of the local community at Rough Rock goes back to the first trading post located at the spot called "tsech'izhi" ("rough rock") by the Navajo. This took place around 1915. This community consisted of those Navajo who lived within approximately fifteen miles of the trading post and did their trading there. The trading post was a place of interaction for the people of this geographic area.

The local community of Rough Rock was further enhanced in the mid-1930s by the construction of a local school for grades one through three. Many of the local people helped build the school, and supported it in various ways, including allowing their children to attend it. The school community amounted to practically the same group of people as that of the trading-post community. The two institutions were situated only several hundred yards from each other.

The local community developing around the trading post and the school was slightly disrupted by the grazing district boundaries imposed by the Bureau of Indian Affairs during stock reduction. These grazing district boundaries put the developing geographic community of Rough Rock into three different districts (four, eight, and ten). These district boundaries are shown in figure 5. The fact that the area around Rough Rock was part of three different districts did not stifle the growing community identity until chapters became important (around 1950) and until chapter boundaries were made to coincide with, or at least not to cross, grazing district boundaries. This development caused the people living in the Rough Rock area to be divided into what is now four different chapters, thus practically eliminating the earlier community identity built around the local school and trading post.

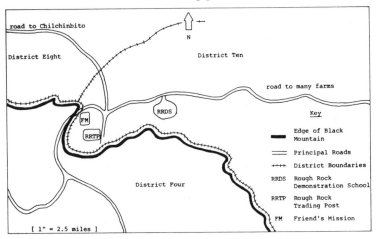

Figure 5. Map of the Rough Rock–Black Mountain area

About five or six years ago, the people of this area (from all chapters) got together and made many requests for a new and larger school. They knew that each chapter by itself could not justify a new and larger school, and so they joined together in requesting a new school. In 1966, a new and larger school was built. As things turned out, it became the first school to be turned over to the local people to be governed by them. Because the officials involved in turning the school over to the community were unaware of local chapter boundaries and grazing districts, the school was in fact turned over to only one section of the people (district ten) who had requested it and for whom it was built.

The result of this outside, official ignorance was a good demonstration (in a reversed sense) of the very thing the school was supposed to demonstrate. The school was supposed to demonstrate the value of local community control of schooling, as well as the problems of outside, expert control. In an ironic way, the outside experts fumbled the ball before the kickoff. They went to the Rough Rock chapter to have the local school board elected. They elected five members from district ten, one of whom came from outside the school district but from within grazing district ten. The people of districts four and eight were not involved in the election, and thus were not represented on the school board.

The school district became identified with the earlier trading-post and school community, but this ran counter to the grazing districts and the political units called chapters. Although steps have now been taken to have representation on the school board from all areas of the school district, community organization and identity remain, to a certain extent, stifled by the confusion of conflicting boundaries. What exists now is a separate community for school matters crosscutting several grazing district and chapter boundaries. The people of Rough Rock have certainly done the best they could, given the conflicting impositions they have received from officialdom.

The area of this study falls totally within the current Rough Rock school district, but it involves only two of the three major sections of the school district. It includes the people who live in districts four and ten. District four includes those who live on top of Black Mountain, and district ten includes those who live on or near the northern and eastern edges of Black Mountain. The Black Mountain area is close to the geographic center of the Navajo reservation. It is more than a hundred miles from any off-reservation town. It can be reached only by dirt road, and is thus one of the more isolated places on the reservation.

Within districts four and ten of the Rough Rock school district, I have chosen fifty contiguous subsistence residential units for this study. The term "subsistence residential unit" may be new to many readers, and so I shall provide a brief description of the social unit to which this term is applied.

The subsistence residential unit is the fundamental unit of Navajo social organization. It is organized around a sheep herd, a customary land use area, a head mother, and sometimes agricultural fields—all of which are called mother. The primary functions of the subsistence residential unit are to provide its members with a place of residence and a source of subsistence.

The personnel of the subsistence residential unit are organized around a head mother. Rights of residence and membership in the unit are based on the primary bonds of kinship (mother-child) and affinity (husband-wife). The first rule of residence gives every Navajo the right to live with his mother, and so the first means of recruitment is by maternal descent or matrifiliation. The second rule of residence in Navajo social organization is that a husband has the right to live with his wife, and a wife has the right to live with her husband. So if a husband wishes to live with his mother, he may do so and bring his wife with him. Likewise, a wife may live with her mother and bring her husband with her.

The personnel structure of a typical subsistence residential unit is diagrammed in figure 6.

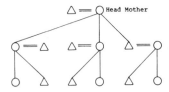

Figure 6. Personnel structure of a typical subsistence residential unit

Members of a distinct subsistence residential unit put their sheep into a common herd and share in the tasks of caring for the herd. The sheep herd is normally the most important cooperative enterprise of the unit. The group or communal life of the unit finds its life and existence in the cooperative economy of the unit. And it is in the sheep herd, more than in anything else, that the divergent interests of the individual members of the unit are converged into this meaningful, cooperative undertaking.

Sheep are individually owned, but are herded and cared for in common within a subsistence residential unit. Nearly everyone has an interest in the common herd, because he or she has his or her own sheep in the common herd. Children are given lambs to begin building their flocks as soon as they are able to share in the tasks of herding, which usually occurs around the age of five. It is in the corporate enterprise of the sheep herd that the Navajo child learns the meaning, necessity, and nature of group or communal life, and it is this experience, more than any other, that forms his social personality.

To summarize, the subsistence residential unit provides a place of residence and subsistence for its members. It is a multifunctional corporation. Its major asset is land. Its major enterprise is usually the sheep herd. Most of its members are stockholders—that is, they have livestock in the common herd. Recruitment is by marriage and matrifiliation. The subsistence residential unit utilizes all the symbols of motherhood in its organization, structure, and integration.

The next three chapters will be concerned with a detailed description and analysis of fifty contiguous subsistence residential units in the Rough Rock–Black Mountain area.

# 9    Residence in the
Subsistence Residential Unit

Residence rules and patterns in Navajo social organization have not been adequately described, and much confusion has arisen about them. The Navajo are most often described as preferably matrilocal in residence patterns. Nearly everywhere matrilocal residence has been found to be more common than patrilocal residence, but some patrilocal residence has been found in every area of the Navajo reservation. To say that the Navajo rule for residence after marriage is matrilocal leaves much patrilocal residence to be explained. On the other hand, to say that Navajo residence patterns are bilocal leaves the preference in actual numbers for matrilocal residence unexplained. Although matrilineal descent has nothing whatsoever to do with residence rights, it has sometimes been brought into the discussion of residence rights and has confused the issues.

The reason, it seems to me, that there has not been an adequate description of Navajo rules for residence is that those studying the Navajo have tried to determine these rules from actual patterns of residence and have attempted to describe the rules with inappropriate terms such as "matrilocal" and "patrilocal." From what I have learned from talking and living with the Navajo, residence rules are extremely simple and are based on concepts and relationships discussed earlier in the cultural analysis. Despite this simplicity, there is not a single term in the terminology of social anthropology which accurately describes them.

Navajo residence rules are based on the primary relationships of kinship and affinity. These two relationships are the mother-child and the husband-wife relationships, respectively. A Navajo may live wherever his or her mother has the right to live. A mother has the right to live wherever her mother lived. In addition, a Navajo may live wherever his or her spouse has the right to live. Residence rules are therefore based on the mother-child and husband-wife relationships, and residence rights are acquired from one's mother and one's spouse.

A subsistence residential unit is organized around a head mother. Rights to membership in the unit are derived from the head mother. All her children may live in the unit, and so may her husband. The spouses of her children may also live in the unit. The children (grandchildren of the head mother) of these couples may of course live with their mothers. These rights of residence could be extended on and on, by any combination of husband-wife and mother-child links.

There are two important kinds of breaks in the chain of residence rights based on combinations of husband-wife and mother-child links. One of these is divorce, and the other is death. Both death and divorce in patrilocal residence patterns mean different things, and are resolved in ways different from those in the same occurrences in matrilocal residence. Therefore they will be dealt with separately. In addition, death and divorce occurring in the leadership generation (highest ascending generation) of the unit are different from divorce and death occurring in generations below the leadership generation. These differences will also be noted in the following account of divorce and death as breaks in the chain of residence rights.

When divorce occurs between a couple living matrilocally, the husband returns to his mother's unit, and the wife and children remain. The same is true in the leadership generation, although divorce is uncommon at the leadership level.

If the husband dies, the wife and children remain in the unit with no change in residence. A brother or other close relative of the deceased husband may be encouraged to marry the widow, but this is not required of either party. The same is true for the leadership generation, although here there will not likely be any encouragement to remarry.

When the wife dies, the husband is either expected to remarry into the unit or to leave. If he remarries into the unit, his children will normally stay with him in his household and be cared for by his new wife. If he leaves, the children will be expected to stay, and will be raised by their maternal grandmother or by their mother's sister. This is not true in the leadership generation. In the leadership generation, the husband will be permitted, even expected, to stay without remarrying.

When divorce occurs in patrilocal residence, the wife and the children return to her mother's unit. The husband of course remains with his mother. In the leadership generation, however, it is different. An example from a specific case at Rough Rock will illustrate the difference. Sally married Blue Coat, and they lived at his mother's house. They had a big family. Later, Blue Coat's mother died, and Blue Coat and his wife, with their children, spouses of their children, and their grandchildren, set up a new unit on the land of Blue Coat's mother. Blue Coat's wife became the head mother of this unit. A few years later, they were divorced, and Blue Coat was forced by his wife to leave. Blue Coat went to his sister's unit for a while, and then remarried elsewhere. Sally and her children, grandchildren, and great-grandchildren continue to live on land that was formerly Blue Coat's mother's land. This is unusual only in the sense that divorce is uncommon at this age or generation. The patterns of residence followed in this case are normal and expected, for in patrilocal residence the daughter-in-law becomes the head mother when she and her husband establish a new or separate unit upon the death of the husband's mother or, sometimes, before her death.

If the husband dies, the wife is expected either to remarry into the unit or to return with her children to her mother's unit. She can also remarry elsewhere and take her children with her. In the leadership generation, the wife will remain without remarrying into the unit, because she will likely be the head of the unit.

Upon the death of the wife, the children will most likely remain with the husband in his unit. They will likely be raised by their paternal grandmother, whom they will then call mother.[1] Children living in their father's mother's unit usually address their paternal grandmother with the term "shima sani" ("maternal grandmother" or "elderly mother"). The normal term used between paternal grandparents and their paternal grandchildren is "shinali," which is used self-reciprocally. It is considered inappropriate in a situation where one's paternal grandmother is the head mother of the unit in which one resides. (It might also be pointed out that where cross-cousins live in the same unit, they address each other as siblings and not as cross-cousins. Likewise, father's sisters are addressed as "shima yazhi" ("mother's sisters") instead of "shibizhi" ("father's sisters").

Exceptions to these rules and patterns do occur in rare cases because of either necessity or demand. Where exceptions do occur, they must be approved and accepted by all concerned, particularly by the head mothers of the units involved. For example, if a man has some children by a previous wife and wants to keep them and bring them with him to a new marriage, he must first get the approval of the children themselves.[2] Second, either the mother of the children or their maternal grandmother, if their mother is not alive, must approve. Third, the new wife of the man must approve. Fourth, the head mother of the new unit must approve.

The Navajo preference for matrilocal residence may be explained, in part, by the fact that neither death nor divorce uproots or disrupts the residence patterns of families living matrilocally to the extent that these same occurrences do to families living patrilocally. In addition, the cultural categories show that mothers and daughters are slightly more solidary than are mothers and sons. With these two facts in mind, it is easy to see why Downs came to the following conclusion:

> There is a general tendency to want to live with one's mother after marriage, but more often than not, the wife's desire to live with her mother overrides the husband's desire to remain with his mother (1964: 68).

The actual numbers and percentages of residence patterns among the people of the Rough Rock–Black Mountain area are compiled in table 1. Married couples whose older member is over forty are separated from couples whose older party is under forty. The preponderance of matrilocal residence in the past is illustrated by the data on the over-forty couples. This same preponderance of matrilocal residence is maintained by the younger couples who are continuing to live in traditional subsistence residential units. However, half of the younger couples are living neolocally. Of this group, 45 percent are living off the reservation, and 55 percent are living in governmental, school, or industrial compounds on the reservation, which are developing into small towns or cities.

Neolocal residence is not a new concept or pattern among the Navajo. Before this century, when there was seemingly plenty of land, couples wishing to break away from one or the other's natal unit could do so whenever they wanted to and had enough skill and livestock to make it on their own. Their new unit would be established wherever there was sufficient unused grazing land. In the past, all units moved around considerably in search of better

TABLE 1          Residence Patterns of Married Couples
                 of the Rough Rock–Black Mountain Area

|  | Number | Percent |
|---|---|---|
| *Under forty* | | |
| Neolocal | 60 | 50 |
| Matrilocal | 42 | 35 |
| Patrilocal | 18 | 15 |
| *Over forty* | | |
| Matrilocal | 33 | 79 |
| Patrilocal | 9 | 21 |

grazing areas. As the population expanded and the land became more or less totally occupied and utilized, the opportunities for both moving around and neolocal residence were greatly reduced. Until wage employment became possible for many, there was little neolocal residence.

The most important point about these statistics and many more which I have collected is that the traditional subsistence residential units are continuing to function much the way they have for a long time. At least half of the younger people, however, are not living in these units but are supporting themselves in other ways.[3] But the traditional sheep camps are still functional for many people. Thus, the new economic and residence patterns are not destroying the old patterns; they are just supplementing them. People living out of the traditional units as far away as Cleveland, Ohio, often still have sheep in their mother's unit and, by so doing, maintain contact with, and interest in, the unit. Nearly every Navajo has a "sheep" home and a "mother" land to which he or she can return, if only for occasional visits.

As long as a Navajo's mother is alive, he or she may go anywhere and do anything and still return to his or her mother's unit to live, eat, and help care for the sheep herd. However, at the death of his or her mother, residence rights must be asserted or he or she must forever hold his peace, so to speak. If residence on the mother's land is not established at or before the time of death of the mother and is not maintained after the death, residence rights are soon lost. In other words, if a man is living with his wife outside his mother's unit when his mother dies, he may return (providing there is enough land to make it feasible) to his mother's land area and set up a new unit with his wife as its head, or he may continue to live with his wife in her unit. If he does continue to reside in his wife's unit, he may not later return to his mother's land for purposes of residence and/or grazing.[4] At the death of a head mother, the unit usually divides into several new units headed by her daughters and/or her daughters-in-law.

The possibility of living away from one's mother's unit, and then later returning to it, suggests that there is some switching back and forth between matrilocal, patrilocal, and even neolocal residence. The data which I have collected, even though incomplete, suggest that about 25 percent of all couples have made at least one switch from one residence alternative to another. Some couples have made many of these switches, and a few in the Rough Rock area switch back and forth seasonally. This may continue as long as one's mother is alive.

Because a Navajo may always return to his or her mother's unit to live, there are always a number of members or potential members of the subsistence residential unit who are not residing in the unit. These out-resident members often keep some sheep in the common herd, and thereby maintain their tie to the unit. Out-resident members can be divided into two main types: temporary out-residents, and permanent out-residents. Temporary out-residents are those who have definite plans and times set for their return to the unit. This type involves mostly boarding-school students, college students, members of the armed services, and those away on seasonal farm work.

Permanent out-residents are those who have no definite plans or times for returning to the unit but who can return if they so desire. These are usually those who have married into other units and are living there, those who have permanent jobs off the reservation, or those who have jobs and homes in various governmental operations or other such establishments on the reservation. Of the 957 members of the fifty subsistence residential units included in this study, 385 (40 percent) were in-residents, 295 (31 percent) were temporary out-residents, and 277 (29 percent) were permanent out-residents. This distribution is shown in table 2.

These figures do not take into account the fact of dual membership or dual residence rights. A family living as in-residents in one unit may well be permanent out-residents of another. This is because one may switch one's residence to the home or natal unit of the spouse at whose home unit one is not currently living. Also, permanent out-residents living off the reservation can return and become in-residents. The figures above represent the current

TABLE 2        Distribution of Residents in Fifty
               Contiguous Subsistence Residential Units

|  | Number | Percent |
|---|---|---|
| I. Permanent in-residents | 385 | 40 |
| II. Temporary out-residents | 295 | 31 |
|    A. Boarding-school students (281) |  |  |
|    B. College students (8) |  |  |
|    C. Armed forces (4) |  |  |
|    D. Seasonal farmwork (2) |  |  |
| III. Permanent out-residents | 277 | 29 |
|    A. Compound housing on reservation (119) |  |  |
|    B. Living off the reservation (102) |  |  |
|    C. Living in traditional SR units out of area covered in the study (56) |  |  |

primary position of the 957 persons involved in the fifty units studied. Therefore, at the time of the study, there were 385 persons living in the fifty units, 295 temporarily living outside of the fifty units (mostly boarding-school students), and 277 potential in-residents living outside the fifty units. (This number includes the spouses and children of those who were born and raised in one of the fifty units, because these spouses and children are also potential residents of the fifty units.)

Of the 385 in-residents shown above, 114 have residence rights in another unit within the fifty, and can be considered permanent out-residents of those units. This results from individuals of one unit being married to individuals of another. These couples and their families are in-residents in one unit—the place of their current home—and out-residents of another. Another large percentage of the 385 current in-residents are potential residents of a number of units outside the fifty involved in the study. This results from persons outside the area marrying into one of the fifty inside the area of this study.

The features of dual residence rights and dual membership are confusing for those who like to put each person in a single slot, as I have done in the chart above. However, if we are truly to understand how the Navajo social system works, we must consider and deal with the dimension of dual residence rights, as I have tried to do in the two preceding paragraphs and in the earlier part of this chapter. As mentioned earlier, the incomplete data which I have collected indicate that approximately 25 percent of all married couples switch their residence at least once during their marriages, and a few do so more often.

The average number of in-residents in the fifty units studied is 7.7 persons. The average of temporary out-residents is 5.9 persons, and the average of permanent out-residents is 5.5 persons. This makes a total average of 19.2 persons per unit. The actual range in total membership for a unit varies from three to forty-eight. The range of in-residents varies from one to thirty-three. The range of permanent out-residents varies from zero to twenty-six. By assuming that boarding-school students are one-third dependent on their units, an average of ten persons actually depend on the economy of the unit for their livelihood.

Another interesting fact is that of those persons who were born in one of the fifty units and are now married and residing in a traditional subsistence residential unit, 61 percent married into one of the other fifty contiguous units, another 27 percent married into units within twenty-five miles of Rough Rock, and only 12 percent married into units more than twenty-five miles from Rough Rock. This indicates that there are many marriage ties linking the fifty units. This matter will be dealt with in greater detail in chapter 8.

TABLE 3      Data on the Ages and Sex of In-Residents
             and Temporary Out-Residents

| Age Group | Number | Percent of Total |
|---|---|---|
| 0–20 years | | 63.6 |
| Male | 217 | 31.9 |
| Female | 215 | 31.7 |
| 21–40 years | | 17.6 |
| Male | 49 | 7.2 |
| Female | 71 | 10.4 |
| 41–60 years | | 12.8 |
| Male | 37 | 5.4 |
| Female | 50 | 7.4 |
| 61–93 years | | 6.0 |
| Male | 24 | 3.5 |
| Female | 17 | 2.5 |

The distribution of age and sex among the 680 in-residents or temporary out-residents is shown in table 3. Temporary out-residents are almost exclusively boarding-school students, of whom almost all are in the 0 to 20 age category. This means that those above twenty are nearly all in-residents. The permanent out-residents, if included, will mostly fall into the two under-forty categories, for most of them are young families with young children. One of the striking aspects of these figures is the predominance of females in the two categories between twenty and sixty. I think this reflects the fact that the roles of women in the subsistence residential unit remain strong, firm, and important, while many of the traditional roles of young men are decreasing in importance and demand. This would be particularly true of the roles of hunter and warrior. Thus, young men are in search of new roles of importance and fulfillment. These are usually found in wage work, and wage work usually means residence outside traditional subsistence residential units.

The role of leader of the subsistence residential unit is still normally a function of men, but these men are usually older and most often the husband of the head mother. If the head mother has no husband or if he is dead, the oldest son or the husband of the oldest daughter will normally be the leader. The leadership role, like that of the role of head mother, is not a role for which the Navajo have a specific title. But in every unit there is a person, usually a man, who takes the lead in directing and conducting the affairs of the unit. This role in particular entails taking the lead in livestock operations—sheep, cattle, and horses—and in agricultural operations. In addition, the leader is the one who deals with the outside world, meaning that he speaks for the unit at community meetings, negotiates with the traders and car salesmen, arranges marriages and ceremonies, talks to visiting strangers, and so on.

The head mother is the person around whom the unit is organized. She is identified with the land, the herd, and the agricultural fields. All residence rights can be traced back to her, and her opinions and wishes are always given the greatest consideration and usually prevail. In a sense, however, she delegates much of her role and prestige to the leader of the unit. If we think of the unit as a corporation, and the leader as its president, the head mother will be the chairman of the board. She usually has more sheep than the leader does. Because the power and importance of the head mother offer a deceptive appearance to the observer, many students of the Navajo have failed to see the importance of her role. But if one has lived a long time in one of these units, one soon becomes aware of who ultimately has the cards and directs the game. When there is a divorce between the leader and the head, it is always the leader who leaves and the head mother who remains, even if the land originally belonged to the mother of the leader.

Of the fifty units involved in the study, thirty-four (68 percent) had a leader who was the husband of the head mother. In seven (14 percent), the head mother was also the leader, mainly because there was no older, capable man to fill the role. In three cases (6 percent), a son-in-law was the leader, and in another three (6 percent), the leader was a brother of the head mother. (It is abnormal for a brother and sister to share the leadership of a single unit, but this is sometimes required because the land base of the unit is so small that it is not feasible to split the unit after the death of a former head mother.) In two cases (4 percent), a son of the head mother was the leader of the unit.

In the remaining one case the father of the head mother was the leader of the unit. Actually in this case, the father was the leader, and his wife was the former head. After his wife died, the role of head mother went to her eldest daughter, and the husband remained leader of the unit. When he dies, the husband of the current head mother will likely become the new leader of the unit.

Although the roles of leader and head mother and the more general lines of authority usually follow the hierarchical order of generation and sibling order, this is not always the case. Where someone is considered incapable or lacks the respect of others, someone else will fill the role by a sort of silent acclamation. The collective will and feelings of the unit are more often sensed than spoken. More will be said about this in a later chapter. Of the fifty units studied, the number of generations in each unit varied from one to five. The tally for each of the units is shown in table 4.

The personnel of the subsistence residential units are subdivided into a number of households. A household is organized around a

TABLE 4    Generation Structure of Fifty Subsistence Residential Units

| Number of Generations | Number of Units Having Such a Structure | Percent |
|:---:|:---:|:---:|
| 1 | 1 | 2 |
| 2 | 17 | 34 |
| 3 | 21 | 42 |
| 4 | 10 | 20 |
| 5 | 1 | 2 |

mature woman. Normal members of a household group are the husband and unmarried children of the woman. Seldom do two married couples share the same household, unless they have more than a one-room house. Membership in particular households can normally be distinguished by where one eats and sleeps. In the routine of daily life, each household group eats at a separate table in or just outside its housing unit (hogan, log house, stone house, or something similar). During special occasions and ceremonies and just after a sheep has been butchered, all resident members of the subsistence residential unit eat together.

One cannot necessarily determine the number of household units that exist in a particular subsistence residential unit by counting the number of houses or hogans. One household group may have several houses. As one might expect, household units also have a tendency to merge in the winter and to disperse in the summer, generally because of the great difficulty in heating so many separate housing units. If firewood gets extremely scarce or difficult to obtain, the whole unit may merge into the largest, most easily heated housing unit.

Table 5 shows the number of households in each of the fifty subsistence residential units. Of the 117 total households, eighty-four (72 percent) have just one married couple, thirty (25 percent) have no married couples, and only 3 (3 percent) have two married couples living in the same household. Ninety-one (78 percent) of the households are two-generation households. Sixteen (13 percent) are three-generation households, and ten (9 percent) are only one-generation households.

TABLE 5    Number of Households in Each of the Fifty Subsistence Residential Units

| Number of Households | Number of Units Having Such Number of Households | Percent of Total |
| --- | --- | --- |
| 1 | 15 | 30 |
| 2 | 13 | 26 |
| 3 | 13 | 26 |
| 4 | 8 | 16 |
| 5 | 1 | 2 |

This account and data should give the reader a good picture of the residence patterns and personnel structure of the Navajo subsistence residential unit. Future chapters will deal with the ways in which these units fulfill the needs of subsistence, the ways in which unity is achieved and decisions are made, and the kinds of links and ties that exist between and among the various units.

# 10     Subsistence in the Subsistence Residential Unit

The subsistence residential unit, as its name suggests, is the social unit in which or through which the Navajo fulfill their basic needs of subsistence. The main resources on which the subsistence residential units in the Rough Rock–Black Mountain area depend are sheep, cattle, agriculture, wage work, welfare assistance, payments for medical practice, weaving, and seasonal or part-time work. Each of these aspects of subsistence will be dealt with separately and then summarized at the end of the chapter.

Although the sheep herd produces only about one-fourth of the total income of the subsistence residential units at Rough Rock, it is still the most important aspect of the economy of the unit. Some units do not have any cattle, wage workers, agricultural fields, welfare assistance, medicine men, or seasonal workers, but all units have a sheep herd. In fact, the subsistence residential unit is organized around the cooperative enterprise of the sheep herd. Downs notes the following:

> Although in a classic economic sense, livestock is not a dominant factor, it is in fact the directing principle of the lives of almost all the people who live in Black Mesa. Their activities are molded to suit the needs of herdsmen. (1964: 18.)

When Werner and Begishe (1968: 105) asked their informants what they think about most, the reply was nearly always, "the sheep." Reichard further verifies this emphasis upon sheep:

> The Navajo, particularly the women, are "sheep-minded." From the first white crack of dawn to the time when the curtain of darkness descends they must consider the sheep. Yes, and even beyond. (1936: 67.)

The "beyond" to which Reichard was referring was the night when one must be careful that the sheep do not get out of the corral and wander away or get harmed by coyotes. In addition, lambing time requires a night vigil in which one must make sure that the newborn lamb suckles properly and does not freeze.

The sheep herd is a symbol of the life, wealth, vitality, and integration of the subsistence residential unit. Although the sheep are individually owned, they are herded in common within each unit. Everyone in the unit has an interest in the well-being of the herd, and everyone is expected to share in the tasks of herding, dipping, lambing, and shearing. Downs also observed this identification of the subsistence residential unit with the sheep herd:

> I have shown earlier that one of the principles of social organiza-
> tion in the Pinon area is the need to care for individual livestock
> through the cooperative effort of several related owners. This
> relationship between the family and the herd is one tinged with
> rather deep emotion and a great deal of symbolism. Sheep are not
> only wealth in an objective sense but serve as a measure of family
> well-being on a more abstract level of discourse. One is quickly
> impressed with the identification between "the family" and "the
> sheep." (1964: 91.)

All the fifty units covered in this study were organized around a sheep herd was 131. Of the forty-six herds on which I have data, was approximately four thousand acres, and the average size of a sheep herd is 131. Of the forty-six herds on which I have data, seventeen had less than a hundred sheep. Seventeen had between one hundred and two hundred sheep. Ten had between two hundred and three hundred sheep, while two had more than three hundred sheep.

Downs reports that in 1964 each sheep would produce about nine dollars annual income (1964: 16). By taking some inflation into account, this figure would likely be around ten dollars in 1970. This means that an average herd of sheep would produce an average annual income of $1,310. Downs found the sheep-human ratio at Pinon to be 9.2 sheep per person. I found the sheep-human ratio at Rough Rock to be 9.6.[1] This meant that the per capita annual income from sheep was about $96. The total annual income from sheep of the fifty units was approximately $65,500. Although these figures do not adequately reflect the tremendous importance of sheep in the Navajo social system, they do show that the sheep herd is a fundamental aspect of the subsistence feature of the subsistence residential unit.

The individual ownership of sheep has several important features and functions. When the residential group divides or when one person or family leaves the natal group, the sheep are divided among the people according to individual ownership. In the autobiography *The Son of Old Man Hat*, there are several examples of this: "Sometime after this my mother and father got into a quarrel.... Then she went out and separated her sheep and goats from my father's herd" (Dyk 1938: 17.) When his sister and her husband left the group, the Son of Old Man Hat said: "They separated their sheep and goats ... and moved away" (1938.)

Another aspect of individual ownership is the right of disposal or sale. One may sell one's sheep whenever one pleases, and the proceeds are one's own. One is, however, always expected to use a large portion of all one's individual income (including wage work) for the general welfare of the group. When a relative from another group (possibly from one's natal group) comes to one for assistance or for food for a ceremonial performance, one must help by giving one's own sheep and not somebody else's.

The sharing of food is a symbol of solidarity. When a sheep is slaughtered for food, everyone in the unit gets what he or she wants and needs. It would be an antisocial act of enormous proportions for one household to butcher one of their own sheep and not share it with others in the unit. In other words, sheep as sources of food are communally utilized, and the sharing of food is a primary social obligation. This extends even to outsiders and to non-Navajo who may be present at the time of butchering or at mealtime. The refusal to share food is a denial of kinship, and one of the worst things to be said about a person is, "She refused to share her food" or "He acts as though he had no kinsmen"—meaning about the same thing.

Once while I was principal teacher of a preschool operation, I had a parent come to me to ask that one of the teacher aides be fired. The parent said that she had been at the aide's home while the aide and her husband were butchering a beef and that they refused to give her any of the meat. The parent said that any person who acted like that should not be teaching the younger children, and the community nearly dismissed the aide over the incident. The aide saved her job by explaining that the beef belonged to her husband who was Anglo, and that he did not want to share it and did not understand the Navajo attitudes toward sharing food.

Individual ownership always comes into play when one is acting as an individual with regard to a relationship outside the unit or in isolation from it. Communal use, on the other hand, involves roles and relationships internal to the unit. The sale or use of wool is done on a group, not on an individual, basis. The common interest in, and use of, the sheep herd is thus a major factor in uniting and integrating the attitudes and behavior of the individual members of the unit.

Sheep are also an important aspect of the way in which an in-marrying affine is integrated and assimilated into the group. The in-marrying affine may bring a few of his or her sheep with him at the time of the marriage, while leaving most of his or her sheep at his mother's place. As the years go by, children come, and the marriage becomes more stable, the husband will gradually bring more of his sheep to his wife's unit until he finally has all his sheep in his wife's unit. The herd or herds in which one places one's sheep symbolically portray where one's loyalties and interests lie. Sheep are also a symbol of security, and the place where one puts one's sheep is likely to be where one feels most secure. The social identity and position of a given person in the social system are closely tied with one's sheep and their place in a given herd. (It will be remembered that the leaders of most units are in-marrying males.) The words of Tall John, confronting the stock reduction officials, strongly testify to how one's own identity is irrevocably attached to his sheep: "If you take my sheep you kill me. So kill me now. Let's fight right here and decide this thing." (Downs 1964: 20.)

Of secondary but increasing importance in the livestock operations of subsistence residential units is cattle raising. Fifty-two percent of the units at Rough Rock had some cattle. Of the forty-six on which I have data, four had under ten head; twelve had from eleven to twenty-five; three had from twenty-six to fifty; five had over fifty. This averages fourteen head of cattle per unit. If we assume that cattle yield an annual income of twenty-five dollars per head, fourteen head would produce $330 annual income.[2] This is about one-fourth of the income produced by the sheep herd. There is a trend, mostly on the part of men, to use more of their grazing rights for cattle and less for sheep.

Only eight of the units at Rough Rock plant fields. The crops grown are mostly corn, melons, and squash. Most of these are either consumed within the unit or shared with relatives outside the unit. Sometimes a portion will be sold, but not often. The main reason that most of the units do not plant fields is the lack of access to water for irrigation. Those who do plant fields are in a position to capture some of the runoff water from the mountains or from drainage areas elsewhere. These fields probably produce about two hundred dollars' worth of food, but because only one in five units has agricultural fields, this must be reduced to forty dollars average annual income per unit from agriculture.

Wage work at Rough Rock has increased fourfold because of the employment opportunities for local people at the Rough Rock Demonstration School, which began in 1966. This was the first federally built and funded school to be controlled by the local people through a school board. The school board established a policy which gave preference in employment to local people, and in 1970 the school employed thirty-four persons from the fifty units studied. Another ten had jobs elsewhere. This means that there was approximately one wage worker per unit.

In fact, however, wage work is not evenly distributed among the units. Eighteen units have no wage workers; seventeen, have one; seven have two; three have three; and one has four. The estimated average annual income of these wage workers is $4,200. Most of these jobs are nonprofessional or semiskilled, though a few are professional and highly skilled.

There is a general myth, particularly widespread among conservatives, that all Indians live on a government dole. Though the Navajo and other Indians have plenty of reason to expect payments for wrongs committed against them by the United States and its non-Indian citizens, no such payments exist. Navajo pay all taxes that non-Navajo pay (except property tax on reservation land), and they get no welfare assistance that other Americans do not.

There are two sources of income for Navajo in this area. One is aid to dependent children for women with children and without husbands. The other is old age pension through Social Security, which Navajo pay into just as do other Americans. Fifty-six percent of the units at Rough Rock have no one receiving aid to dependent children, and seventy percent have no one receiving old age pension. In the nineteen units which do have women receiving aid to dependent children, there are sixteen with one woman each and three with two women each receiving such assistance. There are thirteen individuals or couples receiving old age pension. There are three persons receiving disability checks. These figures average about one check per unit. I estimate the average annual income per unit from these checks to be $720.

Each of ten units has a medicine man, whose average annual income is probably around $250. Because only one in five units has such a person, the average income from this source per unit is probably about $50.

Weaving is another source of income, and nearly all the units have one or more weavers. I estimate that the average weaver makes $200 per year. With an average of two weavers per unit, the average annual income per unit from weaving is $400. Like sheep, weaving and ceremonial performances contain much more meaning than their economic aspects imply.

The Rough Rock Demonstration School also employs many local people in rotating jobs which last from four weeks to several months. A few from this area also go off the reservation for seasonal farmwork, and a few more are employed on ten-day public work projects of the tribal government. I estimate that there is an average of $240 per unit coming from this part-time work.

The resources of the average unit are shown in table 6. There is an average of 7.7 in-residents, 5.9 temporary out-residents, and 5.5 permanent out-residents. In figuring the average annual income per person depending on this income, the permanent out-residents can be eliminated because they do not in any way depend on the income of the unit. The temporary out-residents are boarding-school students who depend on the income of the unit through the summer, during school vacations, and often on weekends. In addition, parents must provide some of their clothing while they are going to school. Therefore at least one-third of the child's support comes from the unit. By reducing an average of 5.9 temporary out-residents per unit by two-thirds, the average number of temporary

TABLE 6     Resources of the Average Subsistence Residential Unit

| Resource | Derived Annual Income |
|---|---|
| 131 sheep | $1,310 |
| 14 cattle | 310 |
| Agricultural fields | 40 |
| Wage work | 4,200 |
| Welfare and old age assistance | 720 |
| Weaving | 400 |
| Part-time work | 240 |
| Ceremonial practicing | 50 |
| Total | $7,270 |

out-residents depending on the unit for support would be about two. If we add this to 7.7 in-residents, we get 9.7 persons depending on the economy of the unit. By rounding this off to ten persons, the average annual income per person comes out to be $727. This is just below what is often considered the poverty line and, I believe, about one-third of the national average.

If the Rough Rock Demonstration School did not exist or did not help the local people as it does, the average annual income per unit would probably be $4,020. This would reduce it to almost half of what it currently is; so the school plays a major role in the economic life of the community.

The average taken alone can be deceiving in some ways. Although, according to Navajo standards, the average is reasonably good, there is a great range in income among the units. A few units can go as high as $20,000, while other units are as low as $600. Of course the population of these units also varies widely, with one unit having only three members and another, forty-eight. By comparing the income to the number of people depending on the income of the unit, I found that there were eight units in bad condition, twenty-eight doing reasonably well by Navajo standards, and ten which were doing decently according to national standards or were wealthy by Navajo standards. There were four on which my data were not complete enough to make an estimate.

Although much of the income in each unit goes directly to individuals or to individual households within the unit, those who receive this income are expected to use large portions of it in helping others in the group. Particularly, he or she must buy food for everyone or at least share with everyone the food he or she does buy. This extends to many other things as well, such as giving others free rides, bringing them firewood and water, buying them new clothes, assuming a large part of the financial burden of having ceremonies or "sings" at the unit.

This drain on an individual's income from wage work sometimes encourages the individual to leave and find residence elsewhere— most likely off the reservation. But this is not always true, because the individual knows that should his own income falter he will always be helped by others in the group. The added security of the communal life is often judged to be worth the drain on one's own income. In addition, one's unit involves one's home, one's land, one's sheep, one's mother, one's relatives, and one's native way of life. And it should not be forgotten that a Navajo gets great satisfaction and inner comfort from helping his or her relatives and being a good member of the group.

# 11    Unity in the Subsistence Residential Unit

The unity of the subsistence residential unit is based on a unique combination of individualism and communalism. According to Navajo cultural beliefs, each being in the world has the right to live, to eat, and to act for itself. These rights to life and freedom extend to plants and animals as well as to human beings. Only real and present human need justifies the killing of any animal or the cutting down of a tree. When human need requires such action, a prayer must always be said to the plant or animal, explaining one's need and asking the pardon and indulgence of the soul of the animal or plant to be taken. Even though many Navajo do not actually do this as much as they themselves agree they should, they still deeply feel this attitude in their hearts and minds whenever they are required to use an animal or a plant.

Reichard observed this respectful attitude toward plants:

> The Navajo have a sentimental attitude toward plants, which they treat with incredible respect.... To pick them without taking them into ritual, to let them wither as cut flowers is quite out of order, even dangerous, there being no aesthetic compensation for the fear such sacrilege may engender. (1950: 22, 144.)

With regard to Navajo attitudes toward the unnecessary taking of animal life, Downs notes the following:

> Many observers of the Navajo have commented that in large part their resentment of the stock reduction program was due to the government's allowing thousands of sheep to die in holding pens or en route to the railroads. Such behavior, perfectly understandable in white economic terms, was viewed as utter barbarism by the Navajo and is still spoken of in Pinon. (1964: 93.)

Navajo believe that each person has the right to speak for oneself and to act as one pleases. The mutual rights and duties of kinsmen normally discussed under the concept of jural relations are best described as mutual expectations, rather than obligations. This distinction is a matter of emphasis and degree, but it is very real and worth noting. Desirable actions on the part of others are hoped for and even expected, but they are not required or demanded. Coercion is always deplored.

When an intoxicated person disrupts a meeting or a ceremony, he or she will be persuaded and encouraged to leave, but no one will throw him or her out. Whenever Navajo see tribal policemen forcefully restrain an intoxicated person and put him or her in a police car, they find something revolting and offensive in the actions of the policemen. They feel the rights and integrity of a human being are violated, even though they are happy to be rid of the disruption caused by the intoxicated person.

Downs described this Navajo attitude as a belief in the "inviolability of the individual." He further discusses some of the social implications of this belief:

> Despite close and absolutely essential familial ties, the Navajo remain highly individualistic people. Their primary social premise might be said to be that no person has the right to speak for or direct the actions of another. This attitude creates specific cultural and social responses. In childhood it permits, or rather enforces the pattern of light discipline by persuasion, ridicule, or shaming in opposition to corporal punishment or coercion.... The decision of a four-year-old that he will stay home from or go to, a squaw dance, or to the store with the family is invariably honored, unless acquiescence is manifestly impossible....
>
> Among adults this emphasis on individualism manifests itself in an unwillingness to make a statement that could be considered a commitment of another person. One learns quickly to phrase questions about other people so that an answer can be given by the informant without violating this rule. Brothers and sisters will politely refuse to discuss each other's likes or dislikes, or husbands will profess complete ignorance of whether or not their wives want to attend a squaw dance. This gives an outsider a first impression that the Navajo know very little about one another, an impression that later is seen to be manifestly false. It is simply a violation of Navajo mores to express an opinion for someone else. (1964: 69–70.)

This cultural belief in, or an emphasis upon, individualism is uniquely complemented by a belief in, or emphasis upon, communalism. The ideal of communalism comes most directly out of the cultural definition of the mother-child relationship, which is realized in acts of giving and sharing. The mother-child bond is the primary bond of kinship in the Navajo cultural system, and all kinsmen are essentially mothers and children to each other. If the Navajo have a golden rule, it would be, "One should treat everyone as a kinsman." This ideal is expressed in the fact that everyone, even a stranger, is addressed with a kinship term. The negative side of this is that one of the worst things one can say about another person is, "He acts as if he had no kinsmen."

To most Westerners, the concepts of individualism and communalism are opposite ideological beliefs and cannot cooccur in the same system without producing contradictions and confusion. But to the Navajo, these concepts are complementary and fit together well in their cultural system. Many students of Navajo culture have failed to understand the complementarity of these two ideological concepts.

John Ladd, a philosopher, made a study of the Navajo moral code. He provides an interesting discussion of egoism and altruism in Navajo morality:

> One of the most interesting aspects of the reconstructed Navajo code of morality is the light it throws on the relations between egoism and altruism. Western moralists have generally assumed that egoism and altruism are incompatible; and therefore, that one of them must be rejected. . . .
>
> According to the Navajo ethical system which I have outlined, it is impossible to be a good egoist without at the time being a good altruist. Although all the moral prescriptions are ultimately based upon an egoistic premise, in content they are altruistic. . . .
>
> The basic factual belief which unites egoistic premises with altruistic conclusions is that the welfare of each individual is dependent upon that of every other in the group. What is good for the individual is good for everyone else, and what is good for everybody is good for the individual. (1957: 303-4.)

The particular social group in which the concepts of individualism and egoism converge with the concepts of communalism and altruism is the subsistence residential unit. This occurs most forcefully and profoundly in the enterprise of the sheep herd. The welfare of one's own sheep is intrinsically related to the welfare of the entire herd. In providing good care for one's own sheep, the individual is providing good care for everybody else's sheep, and vice versa. The inviolability and inviability of the individual and one's sheep are both asserted and demonstrated through putting one's sheep in the common herd, and the common herd beautifully symbolizes both the individualism and the communalism of the subsistence residential unit.

The sheep herd provides the major insurance of the group against hunger and starvation. Because food is shared among all members of the unit, the increase or decrease of a single individual's sheep increases or decreases the food supply for all. Thus, doing good for oneself is inseparably related to doing good for others. Ladd found this thinking to be basic in Navajo economic theory:

> The Navajo "economic theory" assumes that there is a potential abundance of goods, and that through cooperation the amount of goods will be increased for everyone; in other words, they would deny the basic assumption upon which much of our own economic theory depends, namely, the scarcity of goods. . . .
> No man is thought to be in competition with his fellow. Rather, it is assumed that a neighbor's success will contribute to one's own welfare. (1957: 224, 253.)

Nevertheless, one's individual contribution to one's own success with one's sheep is entirely up to oneself. One is never compelled to care for the herd, help with the shearing, or watch over the lambing. One may sell or dispose of one's sheep any time one pleases, and one may separate one's sheep from the common herd if one so desires. In other words, one's individual involvement in the communal enterprise is voluntary, and so the basic rights of the individual to act for oneself are affirmed. By putting his sheep in the common herd, the interests of the individual become voluntarily attached to the interests of the others in the group. By maintaining individual ownership while at the same time making the sheep herd a communal enterprise, Navajo are able successfully to merge the cultural concepts of individualism and communalism in their most fundamental social group, the subsistence residential unit.

Decision making within the subsistence residential unit also recognizes the rights of both the individual and the group. No group can impose its will on individuals within it, and no individual can impose one's will on the group. In other words, the group can only act if all individuals within the group agree upon the action to be taken. If there is one person who objects, the action cannot go forward until the objecting person agrees to go with the group. In addition, a leader or even a head mother cannot speak for or decide for the group, or commit the time and efforts of anyone in the group without his or her consent. No leader or boss and no majority can violate the rights and integrity of the individual. Group action can occur only through the convergence of all individual interests and wills, and this convergence is again most successfully accomplished through the sheep herd. The unity and integration of the group realized in the sheep herd extend to all aspects and activities of the unit.

If unity is realized in the sheep herd, it is likely that disunity would also find some expression through the sheep herd. It has already been explained that when conflicts within the unit become so great that one or more persons decide to leave the unit, these persons separate their sheep from those of the others. Where disunity does not result in separation, this disunity is expressed or symbolized in specific kinds of behavior with regard to the herd. Downs reports the following:

> However, when the family is torn by interpersonal tensions or openly expressed hostilities for any reason, the care of the sheep herd drops off noticeably. The animals are simply turned out of the pens and left to fend for themselves with only a casual watch being kept. As often as not, they will not be driven to water until necessity forces the move. Once penned in the late morning they may not be taken out in the afternoon at all. The job of herding may be assigned entirely to the children, with an attendant series of derelictions. In short, as a focus of cooperation the sheep herd serves as a means of expressing both affection and hostility towards one's close relatives. (1964: 92.)

An important aspect of both unity and disunity in the internal operation of the subsistence residential units is the way in which feelings, attitudes, and decisions are sensed rather than verbally expressed. Serious matters are seldom dealt with at the level of speech, and important decisions are seldom discussed. Decisions are felt and sensed before they reach a verbalized conclusion. Intense emotions, whether affective or hostile, are seldom verbalized but are sensed and/or expressed in various kinds of behavior.

Navajo who live and work together closely for many years learn to communicate with each other without the use of language. Language is for humor, for routine and practical matters, and for communicating with outsiders. Whereas in community meetings, issues are discussed thoroughly before a decision is made, decisions made within the subsistence residential unit involve a minimum of verbal discussion. The problem or issue is usually stated or indicated in some manner, often indirectly. Then there is silence, which is often broken by discussing some other, more trivial matter. In the meantime, thinking and discussion go on at the nonverbal level until someone feels the sense of the group. The time lapse here may be from a few minutes to a few months, depending on the nature and urgency of the matter. The person who has the sense of the group will then suggest the action to be taken, and everyone will likely agree. If someone does not agree, the discussion will go back to the nonverbal level until the objector decides to break it by either agreeing with the formerly suggested action or by suggesting another which he feels will be acceptable to the group.

Silence is also used in dealing with strangers. As the ambivalence and distrust of one's relationship to a stranger are gradually broken down, verbal communication gradually increases from silence to open discussion. As the relationship becomes more intense and familiar, the use of language decreases again, at least with regard to intense emotional matters or matters of serious consequence. Feelings and emotions on these matters are seldom discussed on the verbal level.

# 12    The Navajo Outfit as a Set of Related Subsistence Residential Units

Nearly all accounts of Navajo social organization have attempted to identify and describe some social group larger than the residence group. Kluckhohn used the term "outfit" (Kluckhohn and Leighton 1962: 109); Kimball and Provinse suggested "land use community" (1942), and Malcolm Collier (1951) preferred "cooperating unit." William Adams (1958) suggested that "resident lineage" was appropriate for describing groups at Shonto. Aberle has used "Local Clan Element" (1961), but this presumably refers to a group larger than the ones identified by the previous terms mentioned. Because few maps of residential units or full accounts of the personnel of these units and their genealogies have been published, it is difficult to determine the exact nature of the groups.

There is no specific Navajo term for a unit larger than the residence group; nor is there any such specific term for the household or subsistence residential unit. There are of course various ways in which a Navajo can talk about these groups and make reference to them. Without a specific Navajo term to use, I am left with the choice of using one of the previously used terms or selecting a new one. Because I have already used a number of new terms and because Kluckhohn's description of the "outfit" seems close to the groups which I will describe, I have decided to use the term "outfit," though I will attempt to define it more carefully. Kluckhohn and Leighton provide the following information about the outfit:

> This Western term is used to designate a group of relatives
> (larger than the extended family) who regularly cooperate for
> certain purposes. . . . The differential of "outfit" and extended
> family are twofold: the members of the true Navajo extended
> family always live within shouting distance of each other, whereas
> the various families in an "outfit" may be scattered over a good
> many square miles. . . .

> The variations in the size and composition of "outfits" are infinite. . . . Sometimes the members of an outfit live on lands that have unbroken geographical contiguity. In this case the "outfit" constitutes a "land use community" which may occupy from 12,000 to 80,000 acres and include from fifty to two hundred persons. (1962: 109–10.)

The three largest outfits in the area of my study include from eleven to twelve subsistence residential units, from 111 to 182 persons, and from forty thousand to sixty thousand acres of land. What I call an outfit is a set of subsistence residential units which are subdivisions of an earlier and larger unit. All personnel of the outfit can trace their relationship back to the head mother of the original unit from which the current residential units have sprung. The intensity of the bond between two subsistence residential units is, to a great extent, proportionate to the generational distance between the current head mothers of each and the original head mother. An example will help clarify this.

In figure 7, a subsistence residential unit is shown, with Mary as its head. When Mary dies, the unit will likely subdivide into three units with Susie, Jane, and Carol as the new matrifocal heads. These three new units will retain some important ties with each other, and will be situated on contiguous land areas. They will in fact be a simplified example of an outfit. They will also likely be a relatively intense or closely bound outfit, because the heads of these new units, with the exception of Carol, are daughters of the original head and thus only one generation removed from her. In Carol's unit, the bond will not be so close, because her tie to the original head mother

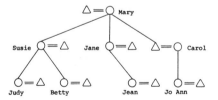

Figure 7. Genealogical structure of a typical outfit

involves two links: one of marriage, and one of matrifiliation. When Susie, Jane, and Carol die, new units may be formed around Judy, Betty, Jean, and Jo Ann. These four new units will continue to be an outfit, because they will still likely be able to trace the history of their unit and their own relationships back to the original unit formed around Mary as its head mother. Being two generations removed from Mary and the original unit, these four new units will not be so closely bound together as the earlier units formed around Susie, Jane, and Carol will have been. Nevertheless, as long as the personnel of two or more subsistence residential units can by memory trace their relationship back to an original unit and its head mother, they will consider themselves to be closer to each other than they are to subsistence residential units with which they have no such connection. In addition, the residential units of the outfit will likely be situated on contiguous land areas.

The functions of the outfit are important, but nowhere nearly as important as those of the subsistence residential unit. Other units within one's outfit may be called upon to help in staging a major ceremony such as an Enemyway, a Nightchant, or a Mountainway. In times of scarcity and dire need, units within an outfit will likely help each other when they can.

Land-use and grazing disputes are often (more so in the past before grazing committees and tribal courts came into existence) resolved within the outfit, and sometimes there is a recognized leader of the outfit who takes the lead in such matters. In the past, members of the same outfit joined together to protect each other from enemy attacks and raids. Today, members of the same outfit usually share in the cost of a funeral, as they now often have expensive funerals (conducted by non-Navajo) for their departed loved ones.

The outfit, however, does not own or control land. It does not have a cooperative economy; economic cooperation occurs only on special occasions with special needs. The outfit occasionally meets as a group and takes collective action, but such meetings and actions are rare. Although in some cases the outfit appears to be a matrilineage, it is not one, since members of many different matrilineal clans may be included in the personnel.

Of the fifty subsistence residential units covered in this study, thirty-four fall into the three major outfits of the area, ten fall into four smaller outfits, and six are parts of outfits which extend beyond the area covered in this study. Because I do not have data on the outfits of which these six are a part, this chapter will report only on the forty-four units which make up the seven outfits on which I do have relatively complete data. Figure 8 shows the location of these subsistence residential units. The areas of the seven outfits are also identified by the single, thin lines which circumscribe them.

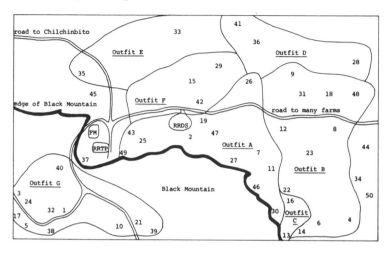

Figure 8. Map of the outfits in the Rough Rock–Black Mountain area

Outfit A covers the area along the northern and eastern edges of Black Mountain. This outfit is made up of twelve subsistence residential units. These twelve units have a total population of 153 persons (including both in-residents and temporary out-residents). The twelve units originated from a single unit formed around Asdzaan Tsi'naazhini as its head and her husband Tachiinii as its leader. This unit was organized about 1890, and continued its existence until about 1915, when four new units were formed. Figure 9 shows the persons around whom the four new units were formed. These were: (1) the two wives of Dine Ts'osi, (2) Asdzaan Yoo'o, (3) Hastiin T'iisbai Sikaadnii Be'esdzaan, and (4) Asdzaan (Tso) Honaghanii. These four units were in existence from approximately 1915 to 1950. The reason for this great period of time is that the four earlier units divided into the current twelve units at various times.

Tsi'naazhini Binanit'ahi (meaning leader of the Tsi'naazhini people) was the recognized leader of this outfit during his lifetime (he died in 1950). His unit is said to have had about two thousand sheep, two hundred head of cattle, thirty horses, and twenty mules. He knew nine ceremonies, two ways of divination (hand trembling and star gazing), and was able to remove objects from the bodies of victims of sorcery. The people say that his material and spiritual power came from his "haniih" ("power by means of practical and ritual knowledge"). He was jailed during the days of stock reduction, but the people say that he was able to escape by means of his supernatural knowledge. He was also a tribal councilman from this area for many years. At the time of his death, there was no apparent heir to his position of leadership, and none has appeared since then; so there is no recognized leader of this outfit at the present time.

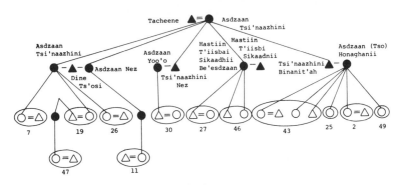

Figure 9. Genealogical structure of outfit A

In figure 9, the couples or siblings (circled) form the leadership generation of the twelve units currently in existence. These genealogical charts are not complete. Only the persons who figure in the relationship of the current units to the original unit are included, and only the leadership generation of the current units is shown. The numbers below the circles correspond to the numbers on the map, so that by relating the two the reader can find all the units shown on this and later genealogical charts.

As with most larger outfits, there are certain subdivisions among the units which are more closely linked together than others. Units 7, 19, 26, and 47 form such a subdivision or subgroup. Figure 8 shows that these four units are situated closely together. There are considerable mutual exchange and assistance between and among them. Sometimes a person from one unit will do the herding for another. Units 19 and 47 sometimes even put their sheep in the same herd for a certain period of time.

One man from unit 19 raised some of his sister's children after her death. These children called their mother's brother's wife "mother," and continue to do so. Unit 47 was established on the basis of residence rights derived from a mother by rearing.

Units 25, 43, and 49 form another subgroup of closely related contiguous units. Units 11, 30, 27, 46, and 2 do not, however, form any kind of closely knit subgroup, but function independently of any close connections such as those which exist among the two subgroups identified earlier. The individual units of the outfit are at least two generations removed from their parent or grandparent unit, and thus the sense of common origin and identity among them is dwindling. Within another generation in the future, it is likely that the new subsistence residential units which will spring from existing ones will be divided into several outfits instead of one.

The eleven subsistence residential units in outfit B all come from an original unit which had Asdzaan Diil as its head and Hastiin Doo Diits'aa'i as it leader. Figure 10 shows that this original unit divided into four new units organized around two daughters (Asdzaan Deezba and Asdzaan Ts'osi) and two daughters-in-law (Asdzaan Tsekehi and Sadie Tahe). Asdzaan Tsekehi was 99 years old when I first met her, and she died shortly after she reached one hundred. Sadie Tahe also recently died. These four units have now divided into eleven units. The population of this outfit is 182 persons. Units 4, 6, and 14 make up a closely knit subgroup. Units 8, 18, and 48 make up another such subgroup, and units 9, 12, and 23 make up a third. In fact, at the beginning of this study, these three units were together in one unit, but in the summer of 1969 they divided into three units. Units 22 and 31 make up another subgroup of this

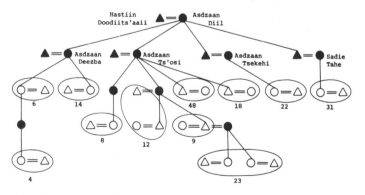

Figure 10. Genealogical structure of outfit B

outfit, but they are not as close now as they were before the deaths of
Asdzaan Tsekehi and Sadie Tahe, who were sisters.

Outfit C is made up of only two subsistence residential units.
These two units are obviously closely related since they form a small
island between outfits A and B. Figure 11 shows the genealogical
structure of Outfit C. The population of this outfit is thirty-three
persons.

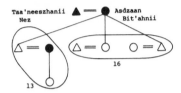

Figure 11. Genealogical structure of outfit C

Outfit D is interesting in that its connecting point is three
generations removed from the leadership generations of the current
units of the outfit. Units 36 and 41 are closest together in terms of
geographical space, but units 28 and 36 are closest together in
genealogical space. Actually, all three of these are independent from
each other, and here the outfit has little meaning. The genealogical
structure of this outfit is shown in figure 12. It has thirty-one
members.

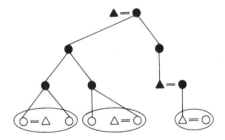

Figure 12. Genealogical structure of outfit D

Outfit E is derived from a couple who settled in the Rough Rock
area about 1930; the head mother was 90 years old in 1970. The two
units are close to each other, and the mother stays for a while at one
place and then returns to the other. Both units are also relatively

well-to-do. The genealogical structure of this outfit is shown in figure 13. Its population is thirty-one persons.

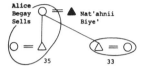

Figure 13. Genealogical structure of outfit E

Outfit F originated in another couple who moved into the Rough Rock area rather recently. From this original unit have come three new units. The three units are situated closely together, and can easily be mistaken for a single subsistence residential unit if one did not observe closely enough to see that there are three separate herds of sheep. The genealogical structure of this outfit is shown in figure 14. Its population is fifty-two persons.

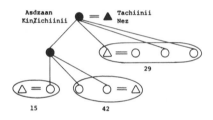

Figure 14. Genealogical structure of outfit F

Outfit G is a large and interesting one, with a long social history. Its former head, Asdzaan Bina'alyahi, was born about 1800. She escaped the trip to Fort Sumner, and died around 1880. She is well remembered through oral tradition by most of the people of this outfit, and nearly everyone can trace his or her relationship to her. The area of this outfit is on the top of Black Mountain which is closest to Rough Rock. Although I show only eleven units in this outfit, there are more than eleven. There are several on which I do not have any data.

Units 5, 17, and 24 make up a close subgroup. Units 10 and 21 make up another such subgroup, as do units 1 and 32. Units 3, 38, 39, and 40 function rather independently of each other. I once observed and participated in the planning and conducting of a Mountainway (Fire Dance) ceremony which was performed by this outfit. At the time (1966), the recognized leader of this outfit was Todecheene Yellowhair. He was the last recognized leader of any outfit in the areas covered in this study. He died in February 1970. He was an outstanding and highly respected man, and the people of this area deeply mourned his passing. He knew many ceremonies, was the instructor of John Honie (another well-known medicine man), and was in great demand for ceremonial performances. The genealogical structure of Outfit G is shown in figure 15. By considering only the units on which I have data, the population of this outfit is 111 persons.

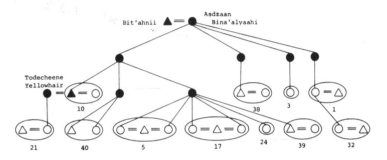

Figure 15. Genealogical structure of outfit G

These data should clearly demonstrate that there is in fact a set of related subsistence residential units which could appropriately be called an outfit. The importance of the outfit has, however, often been overemphasized, probably because the outfit was once more important than it is today. Nevertheless, there is no evidence in the recent social history of the Rough Rock–Black Mountain area that the outfit was ever a landholding or economically cooperating unit. These have always been functions of the subsistence residential units. The main functions of the outfit have been: cooperation in performing major ceremonies; arbitration and resolution of local disputes, mostly land disputes; and mutual economic assistance in times of great scarcity and dire need.

Recently Louise Lamphere has taken issue with the concept of an "outfit." Lamphere argues that additonal fieldwork has convinced her "that the term 'outfit' does not correspond to any group which the Navajo recognize either in terms of their own concepts or in terms of their cooperative activities." (1970: 40.) Her principal evidence against the outfit is that the Navajo have no term for it and that she did not find any outfits at Greenwater. She explains:

> During the course of fieldwork, I became less and less convinced that Navajos discuss cooperative activities in terms of a group similar to an outfit. The difficulties my informants expressed in answering questions about the phrases which I thought might describe an outfit indicated that I was trying to validate a pre-conceived anthropological concept quite different from the Navajo interpretation of social relationships. Furthermore, questions about who should or does cooperate in a particular activity were answered vaguely by phrases like "my relatives" or "everyone helps." (1970: 42.)

Because she did not find an outfit at Greenwater, and because her informants did not answer that those who help them are "members of my outfit," Lamphere looked for some other patterns of ceremonial cooperation. She concluded that "cooperative situations which involve collections of individuals recruited from outside the household and residence group have an ego-centered focus." (1970: 45.) She believes that there are two important variables which divide ego's potential cooperators: genealogical distance, and residential distance.

In genealogical distance, she differentiates between primary and secondary kin:

> I find it helpful to differentiate between primary and secondary kin. Following the usage of Murdock (1949) and of Coult and Randolph (1965: 21), I have defined primary kin as those kin types in a genealogical space radiating out from ego which consist of "two types of units (male and female) that are connected by two basic links (descent and affinity) and a derived link (the sibling link)." These eight resulting kin types are: mother, father, sister, brother, daughter, son, wife and husband.
> Secondary kin are those connected to ego through double primary links. A complete list is provided by Coult and Randolph (1965: 22). (1970: 47.)

Lamphere criticizes others for imposing the concept of an outfit onto the Navajo social system, and then she proceeds to consult Murdock and Coult and Randolph for data on Navajo cultural categories of kinship and affinity. In part I, I pointed out that only the mother-child and husband-wife bonds are primary relationships, and that genealogical distance according to Navajo cultural concepts is not the same as the universal projections of Murdock or of Coult and Randolph.

Lamphere further differentiates between kin living locally (either within the residence group or nearby) and nonlocal kin (those who have moved to other communities or off the reservation). She states:

> The distinctions between primary and secondary, local and non-local consanguinal kin is crucial in understanding which of ego's potential cooperators are actually mobilized in particular ceremonial occasions. (1970: 48.)

She adds, however, that "this does not, of course, exhaust all the possible cooperators upon whom ego may call" (1970: 48).

It takes little sophistication to project that an analysis of this kind and according to these categories will prove reliable in the most highly organized outfit in the Rough Rock–Black Mountain area. The categories are so general that they would probably be fairly reliable for cooperative activities in most societies. But the important point which must be made is that Lamphere's data do not support the conclusion that there is no such thing as an outfit. On the other hand, the existence of an outfit does not mean that there are no ego-centered cooperating patterns; there are. In enlisting assistance and cooperation for performing major ceremonies, the Navajo will normally exhaust all the alternatives their cultural and social systems provide them.

It is the unidimensional approach or the single perspective which has confused the issues about Navajo cultural categories and social patterns. Navajo culture provides a Navajo with a set of kin categories by which one can realize a set of ego-centered kinsmen, upon whom one may call for assistance. In addition, some of these categories and concepts have been used by the Navajo in the formation and organization of social groups. Most of ego's potential cooperators will fit both into ego-centered kin categories and into social groups such as the residence group and the outfit. A Navajo will also enlist the services of kinsmen who might not be members of one's residence group or outfit, just as one will enlist the services of those who are members of one's outfit but are not kinsmen. Thus there are both ego-centered and group-centered patterns of cooperation.

# 13    The Web of Affinity

In the previous chapter, bonds of kinship between and among subsistence residential units were discussed in connection with the Navajo outfit. This chapter will be concerned with the ties of marriage which exist between and among the fifty subsistence residential units covered in this study.

There are thirty-six marriages which link various units among the fifty studied to other units within this group. These marriage ties are illustrated in figure 16. The lines indicate the unit from which the inmarrying affines came and the units into which they married (this

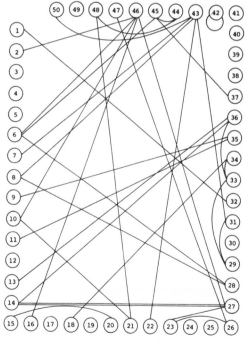

Figure 16. Marriage ties among fifty subsistence residential units

is determined by the place of their current residence). Thirty-five of the units have at least one marriage tie with another unit within the group of fifty.

The strength and intensity of the bonds established by marriage between two groups of relatives are not the same the day of a marriage as they are, say, ten or forty years after the marriage date.

In the Navajo social system, a marriage is normally a gradual process by which an inmarrying affine is separated from his or her natal unit and incorporated into the unit of his or her spouse.

It was shown in earlier chapters that an inmarrying male affine often eventually becomes the leader of his wife's unit, and an inmarrying female affine may become the head of a new unit formed after the death of her husband's mother. Nevertheless, at the beginning of a marriage, the position of the inmarrying affine in the unit of his or her spouse is very tenuous. This is indicated by the fact that usually the inmarrying male affine will bring only a small portion of his sheep to his wife's unit to be put with her herd. As children come and the marriage stabilizes, he will bring more and more of his sheep to his wife's unit. Eventually over a period of from ten to thirty years, he will bring all his sheep to his new unit. By this time he may be the leader of his new unit.

The gradual process by which an inmarrying affine is separated from his or her natal unit and incorporated into his or her spouse's unit can be considered to have three principal phases. In the first phase, the inmarrying affine is attached mainly to his or her mother's unit, and his or her primary loyalties remain there. At the same time, the inmarrying affine is exploring his or her position in the spouse's unit, trying to determine how well he or she fits into the group and how much he or she would enjoy staying in the group for a long time. Of course he or she is also discovering how much he or she likes his or her spouse.

In the past and sometimes today, marriages were arranged by parents and other relatives. Sometimes the couple was married without having seen each other before the day of the marriage. Currently, probably about 75 percent of young couples arrange their own marriages and ask for the approval of their relatives; the other 25 percent of marriages are arranged by their relatives with the approval of the couple. Nevertheless, all marriages are highly tenuous arrangements during the first few years, and divorce is common during this phase.

Sometimes a couple will decide that they like each other and want to continue their marriage, but the inmarrying partner cannot get along with his or her spouse's relatives. In such a case, they may decide to switch their residence to the other partner's natal unit, or they may devise some way to reside neolocally. This most often will mean living off the reservation or in some compound housing on the reservation. It is also possible they can set up their own unit, but this will be rare today because of the scarcity of land. Recently, however, two brothers who are married to two sisters set up their own unit, the oldest person in this unit being thirty-two years of age. Such a move indicates that the marriages of these couples were already well past the first phase.

The second phase of a marriage relationship is a phase in which the interests, loyalties, and bonds of the inmarrying affine are somewhat equally strong or evenly balanced between his or her natal unit and the spouse's unit. It is during this phase that the marriage most serves as a tie or link between the two units involved in the marriage. Children will likely have come by this time, and these will normally intensify the marriage relationship and the relationships between the husband and his wife's relatives and the wife and her husband's relatives.

During the second phase, cooperation between the two units occurs more frequently. The inmarrying affine will be making more of a contribution to the spouse's unit, and the couple will feel free to call upon the wife's relatives to help with a ceremony at the husband's home. At the same time, the husband will feel free to ask his own relatives to assist in a ceremony at his wife's natal unit.

If in the first phase of marriage the inmarrying affine becomes ill and needs a ceremony, he or she will normally return to his or her mother's unit for the ceremony. The spouse will likely accompany in this venture, but few, if any, of the spouse's relatives will be present or contribute to the ceremony. During the second phase, however, the husband will likely have the ceremony at his wife's instead of his mother's home. His mother and many of his other relatives will probably come to the ceremony and contribute substantially to it, as will his wife's relatives. The amount of contact and mutual cooperation between the units is greatest during this second phase.

The third phase of a marriage occurs when the couple becomes the leader and head of the unit or of a new unit. This normally will occur after they have been married twenty or more years and are over forty or fifty years of age. Both of the mothers of the couple will have passed away, or will not be in an active position of directing or leading their units. In this third phase, contact and cooperation between the two natal units of the couple will again be at a minimum, for the interests, loyalties, and bonds of the inmarrying affine will be largely in the spouse's unit and not in his or her mother's unit. All the sheep will be at the wife's unit, and the husband will likely be the leader of that unit. In fact, by this time the natal units of the couple will likely have been dissolved and divided into several new units, and the inmarrying affine will have lost any residence rights on his or her late mother's land.

These three phases in the development of a marriage are not clearly marked by any specific ritual performances or by any conscious declaration. They are merely generalizations of a gradual process by which the inmarrying affine is separated from his or her natal unit and incorporated into his or her unit by marriage. This incorporation involves a new or added relationship between the inmarrying affine and the spouse and the spouse's relatives.

The incorporation of an affine into the unit of the spouse involves a process by which the affine becomes a kinsman as well as an affine. The affine becomes assimilated or adopted into a communal effort, and the communalism of the unit is based on kinship, stemming from the mother-child bond. Involvement in the unit requires the affine to give and share as a kinsman, to begin to address others of the unit with kin terms, as they do to the affine.

For those who think only in unidimensional terms and assume that two persons can be related in only one way, this will be confusing and contradictory. By now I hope I have been able to convince the reader that this is not true among the Navajo. An informant of Shepardson and Hammond made this clear in the following statement:

> . . . . I started living with my present husband; he has never abused me, either with words or physically. . . . In this way I found that if you begin to live with a man as his wife you regard him as a mother to you. You have to depend upon him for sub- sistence. This man was like a mother to me until he lost his eye- sight. I never thought of deserting him because of his condition. I still have a love feeling for him; I stay right by him helping him along with whatever I possibly can. (1970: 168.)

Here a woman marries a man who becomes a mother to her. Then he loses his eyesight, and she becomes a mother to him. Simultaneously they were husband and wife to each other. The Navajo manipulate their cultural categories to make the best of each of the situations in which they find themselves. The above quotation also illustrates how marriage is like acquiring a new mother.

Having discussed the nature of the marriage bond in Navajo social organization, I will now turn to some more concrete data with regard to social organization at Rough Rock. Eighty percent of all marriages at Rough Rock occur between persons of different outfits.

One extremely interesting marriage occurred between two individuals of the same residence group. In this case, a man married into the unit and brought a son from a previous marriage with him. His new wife had a sister about the same age as the man's son. These two grew up together, calling each other brother and sister. When they reached approximately twenty years old, they got married and are still married, living with his father and her sister.

The number of unmarried adults sheds some light on the importance or lack of importance of marriage in the Navajo social system. Thirty-four percent of all the women over twenty-five years of age in the Rough Rock–Black Mountain area are not married. This compares to only 18 percent for the men. The figures for three age groups of unmarried adults are compiled in table 7. Most of these individuals have been married at least once, and are the parents of children. Those under forty years of age will probably marry again.

TABLE 7    Data on Unmarried Adults

| Sex | Age Group | | |
|---|---|---|---|
| | 25–40 | 41–60 | 61–93 |
| Men | 6 of 36 | 8 fo 37 | 3 of 24 |
| | (17%) | (21%) | (12%) |
| Women | 20 of 60 | 16 of 50 | 7 of 17 |
| | (33%) | (32%) | (41%) |
| Totals: Unmarried women =43 (34%) | | | |
| Unmarried men =17 (18%) | | | |

The smaller percentages of unmarried men suggests that men may feel the need to have marriage ties more than do women. In any case, these figures do not suggest that marriage is the articulating principle or the main relationship on which the social system is based, as it is in many societies. The account of the disastrous effects of the separation of the sexes in Navajo mythology serves as a reminder that marriage is, however, necessary for satisfactory social existence and cannot be totally disregarded either by men or women or by social anthropologists.

# 3 Conclusion

# 14    The Social Universe of the Navajo

As already discussed, "dine" is the Navajo term for "people," and thus provides a boundary for the Navajo social universe. Dine are subdivided into two important categories: (1) diyin dine'e—the supernaturals or the holy people, as some have described them; and (2) nihokaa dine'e—the naturals or the earth surface people. The earth surface people are further subdivided into the dine (the Navajo) and the ana'i (the non-Navajo). The ana'i are further subgrouped into various kinds of foreigners or non-Navajo; the dine are further subdivided into more than sixty matrilineal clans, called dine'e—a particular kind of dine.

The taxonomy of the Navajo social universe is illustrated in Figure 17. This may require some explication, because the terms "dine" and "dine'e" are similar, and each occurs at two levels in the taxonomy. This is a simple case of polysemy. The highest or most general meaning of "dine" is "people" or "human beings." The lower level or more specific meaning of "dine" is the "Navajo." If a Navajo needs to clarify to which level of meaning he is referring, he will say "dine bila' ashdla'i" (people with five fingers) for the higher or most general level of meaning, and "t'aa dine" (just Navajo) for the lower or more specific level of meaning.

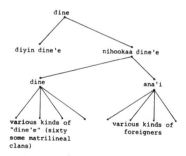

Figure 17. Taxonomy of peoples in the Navajo universe

The suffixing of an "e" changes the meaning of this term to a particular kind of dine. Thus "nihokaa dine'e" is a particular kind of dine. When a Navajo wishes to inquire about the tribe or nationality of a stranger, he will ask "Ha'at'iish dine'e at'e" ("What kind of a person is he?"). He will use the same question in asking what the clan of a fellow Navajo is, which in this case means "What kind of Navajo is he?"

The ideal relationship with all people in the universe is symbolized by the verbal prefix "k'e." "K'e" means "love," "kindness," "peacefulness," "friendliness," "cooperation," and all the positive aspects of an intense, diffuse, and enduring solidarity. At the conclusion of any war, fighting, or confrontation, one often hears the phrase "k'e nahasdįį" which means conditions have returned to "k'e." "Doo k'e nizin da" means he does not think according to k'e, or he is unfriendly, uncooperative, or does not think like a kinsman.

Although k'e is the ideal relationship with everyone in the social universe of the Navajo, this ideal is more imperative and felt more strongly as one goes down the taxonomy to one's own people, one's own clan, one's own family, and, eventually, one's own mother. "K'e" is a general concept of solidarity, and includes both the giving and the sharing of kinship solidarity and the reciprocity of nonkinship or affinal solidarity discussed in chapter 7.

"K'ei" refers to a special kind of solidarity which exists among those related according to Navajo concepts and categories of descent. The suffixing of an "i" on "k'e" is the same kind of linguistic phenomenon as the suffixing of an "e" on "dine." It means in this case a particular or special kind of k'e. Thus when a Navajo says "shik'ei" ("my relatives by descent") he is identifying an exclusive group of people with whom he especially relates according to the concepts and ideals of k'e.

Whereas "k'e" refers to both kinship and nonkinship forms of solidarity, "k'ei" refers only to kinship solidarity based on descent relationships. Ego's k'ei are all those who fall in one or more of the six categories of descent outlined in chapter 5.[1] The Navajo refer to their system of clan or descent relationships as "k'ei yit'ih" (the links of "k'ei" which connect people together). Giving birth is the connecting link to which they make reference, and is the articulating element of the whole descent system. All categories of descent are discussed in terms of how one is born. A Navajo is born by and of his mother and her clan; he is born for his father's clan; he is born together with those who are also born for his father's clan; children of males of his clan are born "for" him; his maternal grandfather's clan are those for whom his mother was born; and, finally, those of his paternal grandfather's clan are those for whom his father was born. It is mothers who give birth, but they give birth for fathers.

"Ba'iishehe" ("those toward whom I marry") and "sha' ayehe" ("those who marry toward me") are the specific ones with whom a Navajo relates according to the concepts and forms of affinal solidarity. "Shik'ei" ("my relatives by birth or clan reckonings") are the specific ones with whom a Navajo relates according to the concepts and forms of kinship solidarity. Because kinship solidarity is the stronger and more ideal form of solidarity, there is an attempt by the Navajo to subsume all relationships under the ideal forms of kinship solidarity, symbolized by the prefix "k'e." As a result, all persons address each other by k'e terms; personal names are never used in address. It is, in fact, very offensive to speak anyone's personal name in his or her presence.

"K'e da'ahidii'niinii" means the "terms we use to address each other according to the concepts of 'k'e.' " This category of terms includes both those used for relatives by kinship and those used for relatives by marriage. To ask a Navajo how he addresses another person, one should say, "Hait'ao k'e bidini" ("How, according to 'k'e,' do you speak to him?"). A typical response would be "shima k'e bidishni" ("My mother—according to 'k'e'—I say to her"). If the relative were an affine of ego, an affinal term would replace the term "shima." Again, however, because the ideal and stronger form of solidarity is that of kinship, Navajo seldom use affinal terms in address.

In identifying and classifying kinsmen, Navajo consider, first, the descent identity of a fellow kinsman. A Navajo considers (1) all those of his mother's clan to be his mothers; (2) all those born for his father's clan to be his siblings; (3) all those of his father's clan to be his fathers; (4) all those born for his mother's clan to be his children;[2] (5) all those of his maternal grandfather's clan to be his maternal grandfathers; and (6) all those of his paternal grandfather's clan to be his paternal grandfathers. This is illustrated in Figure 2.

In addressing relatives by kinship, a Navajo may use terms which identify other attributes of the relative besides his descent identity. In such a case, terms which identify attributes such as sex, lineal or collateral distance, generation, and relative age may be used. The selection of a particular term depends on the number of attributes the speaker wishes to identify. The attributes of sex, lineal and collateral distance, generation, and sibling order (relative age) are used to differentiate relatives in each of the six descent categories. These attributes and their cultural meanings were discussed in chapter 6.

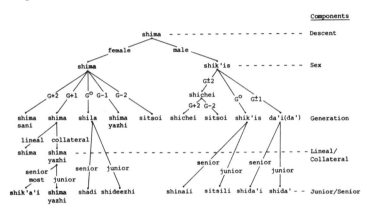

Figure 18. Taxonomy of mother's clan (male ego)

In Figure 18, a taxonomy of terms for those in a male ego's mother's clan are shown. When ego considers only the descent identity of a person in his mother's clan, he will say, "Tł'izi łani dashima" ("Those of my mother's clan are my mothers"). If he wants to take into consideration the sex of the person, he will consider females of his mother's clan to be his mothers and males to be his brothers. If the generational distance from himself is taken into consideration, males of his own generation will be considered "shik'is"; those one generation removed from ego will be considered "shida'i" or "shida"; those two generations removed from ego will be considered "shichei." On the female side, ego first distinguishes lineals from collaterals,[3] and then further distinguishes them on the basis of generational distance from himself. There are still further distinctions made when relative age is considered.

Taxonomies for male and female egos for each of the six categories of descent are presented in Figures 18-24. From these taxonomies it can be easily seen that many of the terms refer to several levels of meaning. For example, the terms "shima" and "shima yazhi" have several levels of meaning. If the genealogical grid were used, these two terms, along with "shik'a'i,"

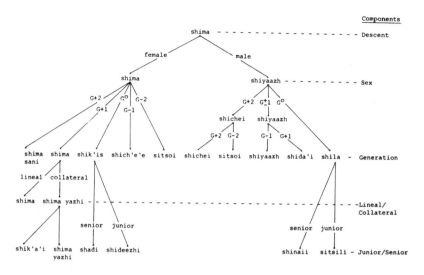

Figure 19. Taxonomy of mother's clan (female ego)

would be listed as alternate terms for mother's sisters when actually they have very distinct meanings. These terms differ from each other in the way they symbolize different attributes of females of mother's clan. "Shima yazhi" may be used to differentiate collaterals from lineals, females of ego's clan who are younger than ego's mother from those who are older than ego's mother, and females who are younger than ego from those who are older than ego. In these cases, "shima yazhi" contrasts in meaning with "shima," which refers to

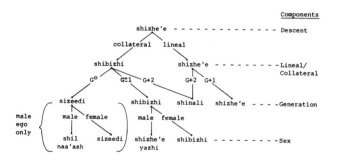

Figure 20. Father's clan (male or female ego)

124    Chapter 14

lineals as opposed to collaterals, females who are older than ego's mother as opposed to those who are younger than ego's mother, and females who are older than ego as opposed to those who are younger than ego. In addition, "shik'a'i" is a term used for mother's oldest sister. These terms and their different meanings are illustrated in the taxonomy in Figure 25.

The taxonomies above present a comprehensive view of the social universe of the Navajo. The solidarity of the Navajo people is based

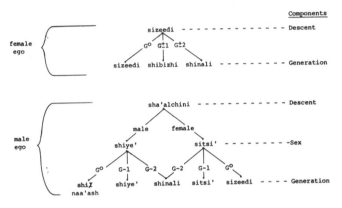

Figure 21. Born for mother's clan

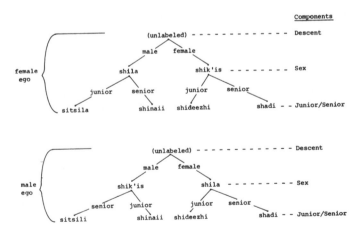

Figure 22. Born for father's clan

on the concept of "k'e," and it is in the mother-child bond that the most intense, the most diffuse, and the most enduring form of k'e is

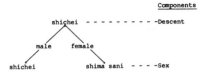

Figure 23. Maternal grandfather's clan

Figure 24. Paternal grandfather's clan

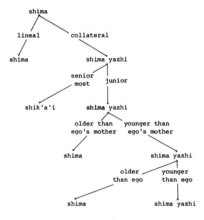

Figure 25. Terms for mother's sisters

found. The solidarity of mother and child, symbolized in patterns of giving life and sharing items which sustain life, is projected in Navajo culture as the ideal relationship between and among all people. All one's kinsmen are simply differentiated kinds of mothers; and, since everyone is treated and addressed as a kinsman, all people are bound together by the bond of k'e. Although as one comes down the taxonomic ladder of the social universe of the Navajo, this bond becomes more intense and more imperative, and although Navajo cultural concepts of sex, generation, sibling order, and lineal and collateral distance further modify this bond in dyadic relationships, the k'e that exists between mother and child provides the foundational concepts and forms for all relationships in Navajo social life. Moreover, this foundational bond of kinship is not limited to people, for the earth is called mother, the sheep herd is called mother, corn is called mother, and the sacred mountain soil bundle is called mother. The symbols of motherhood and the k'e solidarity which they symbolize pervade Navajo culture and provide the patterns and sentiments which order Navajo social life.

# Notes

## Chapter 4

1. It should be added here that Sider (1967: 99–108) found that the Trobriand father was related to his children by both kinship and affinity.

2. I noted above certain difficulties which Leach found with Fortes' concept of "complementary filiation," and I noted also that even with respect to the Trobriand data, which Leach presented, Sider found the Trobriand child related to its father by both kinship and affinity. It is true that both Trobriand and Navajo have been regarded as matrilineal, and the empirical question might arise as to whether this double linkage between father and child in matrilineal systems is also true for the link between mother and child in patrilineal systems. I suggest that this may well be true but that the question depends on a careful analysis of the cultural categories themselves.

## Chapter 5

1. This type of descent category is used as a basis for the Australian section systems.

2. This is also ideally true for those of affiliated clans, but in actual behavior the degree or intensity of solidarity among affiliated clans is less than it is within the same clan.

3. During a community school meeting at Rough Rock I gave a talk in Navajo to local parents about how their children learn to relate to people at the school. I mentioned that children learn the proper way in which to relate to other people through the instruction of their parents and teachers. I mentioned that Navajo parents tell their children not to fool around (sexually) with their brothers or sisters and their cross-cousins. The statement caused a great deal of laughter. After the meeting, five or ten Navajo parents came to me and said that I was wrong and that cross-cousins were ideal sexual playmates. Others denied this, and they continued to joke with each other about it. Although I enjoyed the joking and jesting, I went away a little confused. Later some of the people told me that many Navajo consider their cross-cousins to be their sweethearts and ideal sexual partners but that they really should not do this because their cross-cousins are their fathers, and a girl should not have sexual relations with her father.

## Chapter 7

1. I think this ritual should be called Alienway, but Enemyway is retained here

because it has been used elsewhere in the literature and it would be confusing to use another label.

2. The Enemyway myth can be found in *Origin Legend of the Navaho Enemy Way* (Haile 1938).

# Chapter 9

1. In chapter 6, the analysis of the cultural categories showed that, other than one's mother and one's siblings, the closest kin category is that of maternal grandmother and next to it is that of father. In most cases of patrilocal residence, the paternal grandmother (by genealogy) is really more of a maternal grandmother (by behavioral relationship) than the maternal grandmother (by genealogy). That is why she is more likely to get the children at the death of the mother than the maternal grandmother. Also, the fact that the father is the next closest kinsmen of the children and that he lives in the unit adds greater weight to the likelihood that the children will remain in the unit rather than go to the natal unit of their deceased mother. The reason this situation is described in "likely" terms is that in this case the children are left with no primary bonds from which residence patterns are acquired or determined. By this, it is meant that (assuming they are not married) they have no mother and no spouses. So they acquire a mother—usually the paternal grandmother—and live with her. She will always be their mother, and they will always be able to live with her, even after marriage. In addition, they will always call her mother and not paternal grandmother, unless an Anglo asks them how they are related to her. Then a different set of categories is required. But in the Navajo system, she will be mother through categories of kinship based on action or behavior.

2. Unless they are too young to speak, in which case he will not likely want them or be permitted to take them.

3. Many of these will likely return to their natal units, but some may never return.

4. Grazing rights are traditionally part of residence rights. The grazing permit system instituted by the BIA during stock reduction has, however, messed this up, and sometimes one has residence rights without grazing rights, or grazing rights without residence rights. When the confusion over this gets too great, Navajo usually just ignore the permit system.

# Chapter 10

1. This figure includes in-residents and temporary out-residents (boarding-school students).

2. These 1969 figures are now out-of-date. Current (1974) cattle prices have greatly increased, and the average cash income per head is now probably over one hundred dollars annually. And, as is stated above, Navajo are continuing to raise fewer sheep and more cattle.

# Chapter 14

1. For a man there are two additional categories of relationship by descent. These include his maternal and paternal grandchildren, and are really just reciprocal categories of categories five and six: maternal grandfather's clan and paternal grandfather's clan. That is why they were not listed.

2. This is true for a male ego. For a female ego it is the same except for category four. A female ego considers those born for her mother's clan to be her cross-cousins (zeedí).

3. On the male side, ego has no lineal relatives in his mother's clan.

# Bibliography

Aberle, David F.
1961        The Navaho. In *Matrilineal kinship.* David M.
            Schneider and Kathleen Gouch, eds. Berkeley and
            Los Angeles: University of California Press.
1963        Some sources of flexibility in Navaho social organi-
            zation. *Southwestern Journal of Anthropology* 19:
            1–18.

Adams, William Y.
1958        *Shonto: a study of the role of the trader in a modern
            Navaho community.* Bulletin of the Bureau of Ameri-
            can Ethnology 188. Washington, D.C.: Government
            Printing Office.

Bailey, Flora L.
1950        *Some sex beliefs and practices in a Navaho commu-
            nity, with comparative material from other Navaho
            areas.* Reports of the Ramah Project, no. 2. Papers of
            the Peabody Museum of American Archaeology and
            Ethnology, Harvard University, vol. 40, no. 2. Cam-
            bridge, Mass.: Peabody Museum.

Collier, Malcolm Carr
1951        Local organization among the Navaho. Unpublished
            thesis, University of Chicago.

Collier, Malcolm Carr, Katherine Spencer, and Doraine Wooley
1939        Navaho clans and marriage at Pueblo Alto. *American
            Anthropologist* 41:245–57.

Downs, James F.
1964        *Animal husbandry in Navajo society and culture.*
            Berkeley and Los Angeles: University of California
            Press.

Durkheim, Emile
1933        *The division of labor in society.* George Simpton,
            trans. New York: The Free Press.

Dyk, Walter
1938          *Son of old man hat.* New York: Harcourt, Brace and
              Co.

Eliade, Mircea
1959          *The sacred and the profane.* New York: Harcourt,
              Brace and World.

Firth, Raymond
1936          *We, the Tikopia.* London: Oxford University Press.

Fortes, Meyer
1953          The structure of unilineal kin groups. *American
              Anthropologist* 55:17–41.
1959          Primitive kinship. *Scientific American* 200, no. 44,
              pp. 146–50.

Franciscan Fathers
1910          *An ethnologic dictionary of the Navaho language.*
              Saint Michaels, Arizona.

Frisbie, Charlotte Johnson
1967          *Kinaalda: a study of the Navaho girls' puberty
              ceremony.* Middletown, Conn.: Wesleyan University
              Press.

Geertz, Clifford
1966          Religion as a cultural system. In *Anthropological
              approaches to the study of religion.* Michael Banton,
              ed. New York: Frederick A. Praeger.

Haile, Father Barard
1938          *Origin legend of the Navaho enemy way.* New Haven,
              Conn.: Yale University Press.

Hill, W. W.
1943          *Navaho humor.* Menasha, Wis.: George Banta Pub-
              lishing Co.

Kimball, Solon T., and J. H. Provinse
1942          Navajo social organization in land use planning.
              *Applied Anthropology* 1:18–30.

Kluckhohn, Clyde, and Dorothea Leighton
1962          *The Navaho.* Garden City, N.Y.: Doubleday and
              Co.

Ladd, John
1957          *The structure of a moral code.* Cambridge, Mass.:
              Harvard University Press.

Lamphere, Louise
1969        Symbolic elements in Navajo ritual. *Southwestern Journal of Anthropology* 25:279-305.
1970        Ceremonial cooperation and networks: a reanalysis of the Navajo outfit. *Man* 5:39-59.

Leach, R.
1961        *Rethinking anthropology.* London: The Athlone Press.

Lévi-Strauss, Claude
1963        *Structural anthropology.* Clari Jacobson and Brook Grundfest, trans. New York: Basic Books.
1966        *The savage mind.* Chicago: University of Chicago Press.

Levy, Marion J.
1952        *The structure of society.* Princeton: Princeton University Press.

Morgan, Lewis Henry
1870        Systems of consanguinity and affinity of the human family. *Smithsonian Contributions to Knowledge,* XVII, 1-590.

Newcomb, Franc, Stanley Fisher, and Mary C. Wheelwright
1956        *A study of Navajo symbolism.* Cambridge: Peabody Museum.

Radcliffe-Brown, A. R.
1952        *Structure and function in primitive society.* New York: The Free Press.

Radcliffe-Brown, A. R., and Daryll Forde
1950        *African systems of kinship and marriage.* London: Oxford University Press.

Reichard, Gladys
1928        *Social life of the Navajo Indians.* New York: Columbia University Press.
1936        *Navajo shepherd and weaver.* New York: J. J. Augustin Publisher.
1950        *Navaho religion: a study of symbolism.* New York: Bollingen Foundation.

Schneider, David M.
1965        Kinship and biology. In *Aspects of the analysis of family structure.* A. S. Gale, et al. Princeton: Princeton University Press.
1968        *American kinship: a cultural account.* Englewood Cliffs, N.J.: Prentice-Hall.

Shepardson, Mary
1963            Navajo ways in government. Special edition of *American Anthropologist* 65, no. 3, part 2.

Shepardson, Mary, and Blodwen Hammond
1970            *The Navajo mountain community*. Berkeley and Los Angeles: University of California Press.

Sider, Karen Blu
1967            Affinity and the role of the father in the Trobriands. *Southwestern Journal of Anthropology* 23:90–109.

Spencer, Katherine
1947            *Reflection of social life in the Navaho origin myth*. Albuquerque: University of New Mexico Press.
1957            *Mythology and values*. Philadelphia: American Folklore Society.

Turner, Victor
1966            Colour classification in Ndembu ritual. In *Anthropological approaches to the study of religion*. Michael Banton, ed. New York: Frederick A. Praeger.
1967            *The forest of symbols: aspects of Ndembu ritual*. Ithaca, N.Y.: Cornell University Press.

Werner, Oswald, and Kenneth Begishe
1968            Styles of learning: the evidence from the Navajo. Unpublished working paper.

Wyman, Leland
1970            *Blessingway*. Tucson: University of Arizona Press.

Zelditch, Morris, Jr.
1959            Statistiçal marriage preferences of the Ramah Navajo. *American Anthropologist* 61:470–491.

# Index

Aberle, David F., ix, x, 33
adultery, 26
affine, 114. *See also* in-marrying affine
affinity: nature of, 23-28, 30, 43, 56-57, 127; terms of, 64
age, 48, 121
agriculture, 90
altruism, 96
*ana'i*, 58, 64, 119

biological relatedness, 11
birth, 20, 21, 34, 53
born for, 42, 47, 121
boundaries, 71
bridewealth, 24
buckskin, 62

category, 38
cattle, 89
ceremonial cooperation, 41, 48, 109
Changing Woman, 15, 16, 33
collaterals, 124
Collier, Malcolm Carr, ix
communalism, 73, 89, 94
community, 69
complementary filiation, 29, 38, 127
conception, 24
continuity, 67
cooperation, 108. *See also* ceremonial cooperation
corn, 17, 126
cross-cousins, 46, 52, 55, 127, 129
culture, 3-9

dance, 60
death, 64, 75

decisions, 99
descent: lineal, 39; nonlineal, 39, 44, 48; unilineal, 48; categories, 121, 127, 128
*dine*, 58, 64, 119
distance, 48, 53, 121
disunity, 98
divorce, 75
*diyin dine'e*, 119
Downs, James F., 94, 95
dual organization, 59
dual residence rights, 80
Durkheim, Emile, 5
duties, 94
Dyk, Walter, ix

eagle, 63
earth, 16, 20, 62, 126
Earth Mother, 68
Earth Woman, 61. *See also* Changing Woman
ecological factors, 67
egoism, 96
Enemyway, 57, 127
environmental factors, 67
epistemology, 6
exchange, 28, 56-60, 64. *See also* reciprocity

father, 128
father-in-law, 32
father's clan, 31, 45
female, 17, 24, 50, 63
fertility, 17
fieldwork, x
food, 23, 58, 88
funerals, 102

135